# ADVANCED MODEL RAILROADS

# ADVANCED MODEL RAILROADS

DAVE LOWERY

An Imprint of
RUNNING PRESS
Philadelphia, Pennsylvania

A QUINTET BOOK



9 8 7 6 5 4 3 2 1
Digit on the right indicates the number of this printing

Library of Congress
Cataloging-in-Publication Number
93-70585

ISBN 1-56138-223-X

This book was designed and produced by
Quintet Publishing Limited
6 Blundell Street
London N7 9BH

Creative Director: Richard Dewing
Designer: James Lawrence
Project Editor: Helen Denholm
Editor: Michelle Clark
Photographer: Tony Wright

With thanks to the following for their help with the book:
R.J.H. Model Railways, Parkside Dundas, Victors of London, Brian Monaghan
and Barry Norman.

Typeset in Great Britain by
Central Southern Typesetters, Eastbourne
Manufactured in Hong Kong by Regent Publishing Services Limited
Printed in Hong Kong by Leefung-Asco Printers Limited

Published by Courage Books
an imprint of Running Press Book Publishers
125 South Twenty-second Street
Philadelphia, Pennsylvania 19103-4399

# CONTENTS

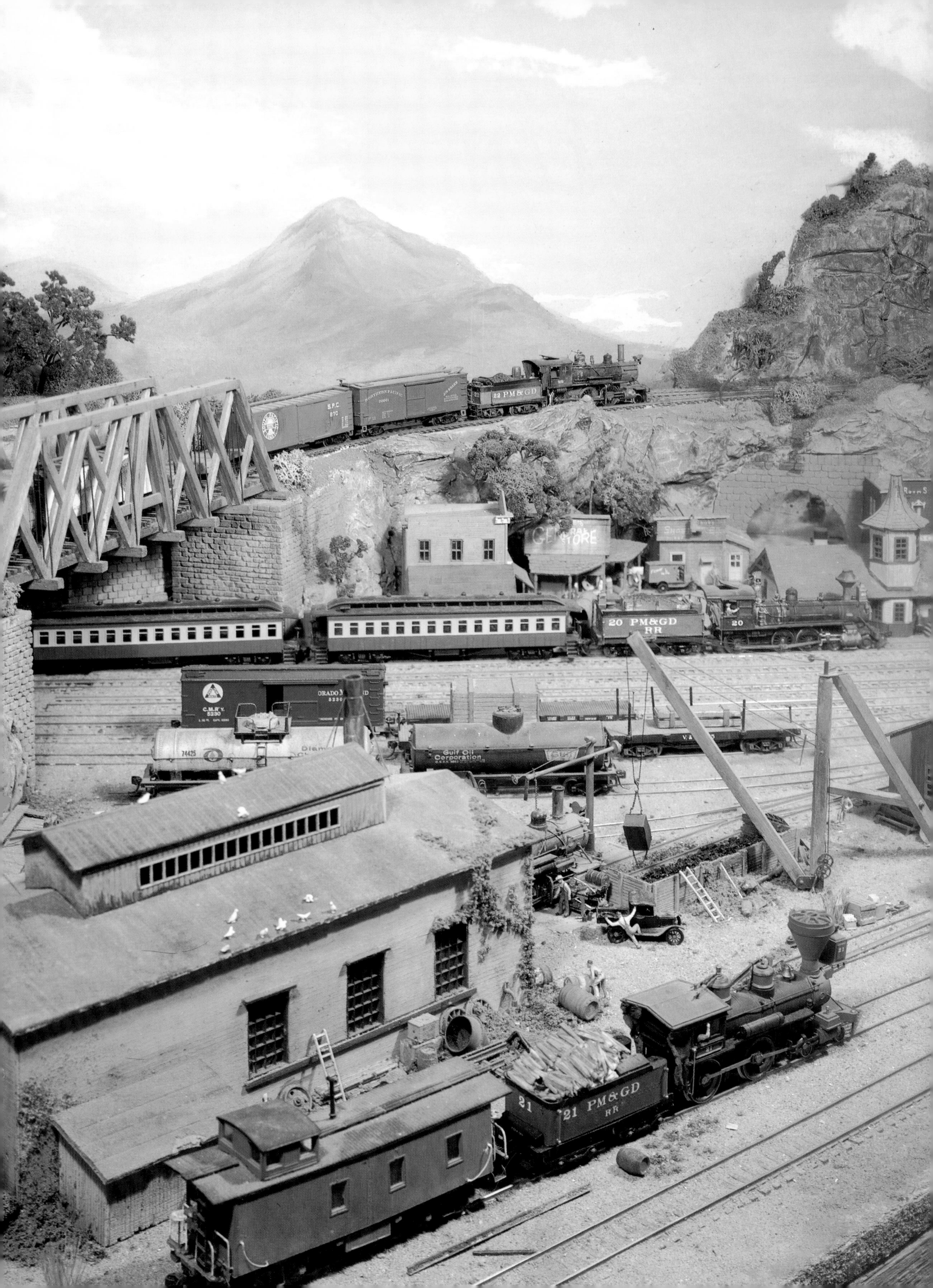

22 PM&GD
20 PM&GD
RR
20
C.M.R'Y.
5230
74425
Gulf Oil
Corporation
21
21 PM&GD
RR

# INTRODUCTION

**LEFT**

**A rocky, barren landcape has been created here as a setting for a fairly involved layout. A realistic backboard has been painted to give the effect of scenery receding into the distance.**

For the model railroad hobbyist who has mastered the basic principles, the next step is to create an individual layout, with its own landscape and features so that it is as realistic as possible. This book provides detailed examples and step-by-step pictures of all the techniques that bring a layout to life.

Methods of base construction are described, as well as how to apply distinctive scenic details ~ from rocks and foliage to various water features and even a wheatfield. Advice is given on the pros and cons of different materials and the color step-by-step photographs show exactly how, for example, realistic grass is achieved by applying not a uniform shade of green, but several shades mixed together.

There are chapters on the stages involved in building freight cars and engines from plastic and metal kits and then painting and lining them, plus the essential final details that make all the difference, such as honest grime and rust. Also included are the various ways in which the architectural details of stations and other buildings can be made.

**RIGHT**

**Two tracks separated by an embankment of grass and scrub. An open-framed base construction will allow you to run lines on different levels.**

After reading this book, you will not fail to be inspired to build your own layout and can be confident that the techniques learned will help you turn your idea into a reality. The world of model railroads is expanding all the time and so the scope for modeling is limited only by your imagination. Look at books, magazines, etc., for ideas and consider making setups of railroads from other parts of the country or from other countries – a train passing through a scene in a film or something you have seen on vacation might provide an idea for a project. Now to the practicalities.

**BELOW**

**This is a complex period layout incorporating four main line tracks and exchange sidings. It might take a modeler a couple of years to complete a layout as detailed as this.**

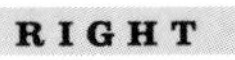

**RIGHT**

This is a view of one side of the finished landscaped base that can be built following the steps in Chapters 2 and 3.

**LEFT**

Find out how to make these O-gauge four-wheel hopper cars in Chapter 8, then, in Chapter 9 how to paint and use masking or lining tapes to create their striking livery.

**RIGHT**

Even a simple base can be interesting. Here a lifelike pond has been added in the corner (see Chapter 6).

PEN-THAVEN BRIDGE
235
SOUTHERN
913
SOUTHERN
2689
5239
GREAT WESTERN
13865
G W
26045
G W
GREAT WESTERN

1

# PLANNING A LAYOUT

**LEFT**

**To add interest, how about a layout where two major railroad companies come together? Here the British Southern and Great Western companies meet.**

When choosing a layout, you must start with a vision of what you want to create and how you want to use it. If, after spending months of hard work building models, scenery, and so on, the finished layout is not satisfying to operate, it will not be interesting for very long. So, purposeful, well-thought-out track routes and controls are vital to a successful model railroad.

In this chapter, basic designing, project types, and a few areas you may not have considered are discussed so that your project will start off on the right foot. Further, without wishing to be too restrictive, it is best that the first layout you attempt is small or at least offers the chance of being achievable in a single lifetime!

There are nearly as many kinds of model railroads as there are railroad hobbyists, so, before deciding what to model, think about what you want from the hobby. Is your chief interest operating the layout, the scenery, or building locomotives? Do you prefer main line, spur line or electric railroad scenes? Do you want to build in the activity of a station or a stretch of line between stations broken by the odd feature? Do you simply need a test track where your latest engine can be put through its paces? Main line scenes require long stretches of track and stations of a certain size to accommodate the rolling stock, so if you prefer this type of railroad, are you prepared for the extra space and extra work that this will involve? Or are you prepared to compromise and use a smaller-scale stock?

Any model railroad that is more than just a test track needs to have a convincing and coherent "story" behind it. This means that the builder must have thought about *where* the line is situated, *why* it was built (for example to carry coal from mines to a seaport or to bring farm produce to a developing town), and what *period* the model is illustrating. From just these points it can be seen that there is immense scope for all sorts of ideas in the area of layout planning. For example, it is possible to model a line that actually exists or has existed, finding out from published histories or local records how the place looked in the chosen period; an imaginary line can be placed in a real location, as long as there is a real reason for the railroad being there; part of a real company can be modeled in an imaginary location (some very fine layouts have been built by modelers who invented not only the railroad but also the town and even the entire country in which it was located).

The important thing is that the railroad should be consistent within itself and true to its surroundings. This may seem a bit pedantic, but if you visit a few model railroad shows, it can be seen very clearly that the best layouts involve the spectator because consideration has been given to all these points.

Many modelers approach their layouts in the same way that a painter does when thinking about creating a scene on canvas, but this medium is three-dimensional. Remember, once you begin to build a scenic layout, you are no longer "playing with a train set," you are building a model railroad. As will probably be clear from what has been said so far, though this is a fun, relaxing hobby, some basic parameters have to be established so that valuable modeling time and effort is not wasted.

Throughout the book are examples of completed layouts to give some idea of what can be achieved, but please bear in mind that a great deal of time is needed to produce layouts to this standard. Do not be disappointed if your first attempt at an advanced layout is not as good as these. No railroad modeler has ever been happy with their first model – but with practice and the experience gained, professional results will come. Therefore, start small, get it finished, gain experience, and put all that valuable learning into the next project.

**BELOW**

**A selection of the most popular gauges, shown at their exact size.**

| Common Name | Scale | G | | B | |
|---|---|---|---|---|---|
| | | in | mm | in | mm |
| 1 | 10 mm/ft | 1¾ | 44.45 | 1.574 | 40.0 |
| 1F | 10 mm/ft | 1.771 | 45.0 | 1.654 | 42.0 |
| 0 | 7 mm/ft | 1.259 | 32.0 | 1.102 | 28.0 |
| 0F | 7 mm/ft | 1.259 | 32.0 | 1.141 | 29.0 |
| S | 3/16 in/ft | 0.875 | 22.23 | 0.781 | 19.85 |
| S4/P4 | 4 mm/ft | 0.741 | 18.83 | 0.703 | 17.87 |
| EM | 4 mm/ft | 0.709 | 18.0 | 0.649 | 16.5 |
| H0/00 | 4 mm/ft<br>3.5 in/ft | 0.649 | 16.5 | 0.570 | 14.5 |
| TT | 3 mm/ft | 0.472 | 12.0 | 0.406 | 10.31 |
| N | 2 mm/ft | 0.354 | 9.0 | 0.291 | 7.4 |
| 2mm | 2 mm/ft | 0.371 | 9.42 | 0.336 | 8.5 |
| Z | 1/220 | 0.256 | 6.5 | 0.216 | 5.5 |

**ABOVE**

**A clear demonstration of a well-thought-out layout on different levels. Rocks have then been filled in between the levels, and a good sprinkling of bridges holds the whole scene together.**

**Back-to-back measurement between the inside faces of a pair of wheels (B) and the relevant track gauge (G), which is the distance between the inner edges of each pair of rails. This table shows which wheel measurements fit each track gauge.**

These completed layouts are here to inspire and to show how varied railroad models can be. One of these masterpieces could contain a certain element that will fire you with enthusiasm and will not let you rest until your own version confronts you in three dimensions!

It might be an idea, if you have not already done so, to join a club, society, or association. This provides an opportunity to look at what a group of like-minded modelers are doing. Also a group can produce a much larger project than can an individual. Most clubs have some sort of running track where first attempts at modeling can be tested and run without having to have your own layout. Do not be upset by criticism, as most of it is constructive and well meant.

**RIGHT**

**The most common gauges with their scales and ratios.**

| Common Name | Scale | Gauge | Ratio |
|---|---|---|---|
| 1 | 10 mm/ft | 44.45 mm | 1/32 |
| 0 | 7 mm/ft | 32 mm | 1/43 |
| *00 | 4 mm/ft | 16.5 mm | 1/76 |
| *H0 | 3.5 mm/ft | 16.5 mm | 1/87 |
| TT | 3 mm/ft | 12 mm | 1/120 |
| N | 2 mm/ft | 9 mm | 1/160 European or 1/148 British |
| Z | — | 6.5 mm | 1/220 |

***00 and H0 gauges are often bracketed together as H0/00 because, although there is a marginal difference in scale, they both run on the same track gauge.**

## Developing a Design

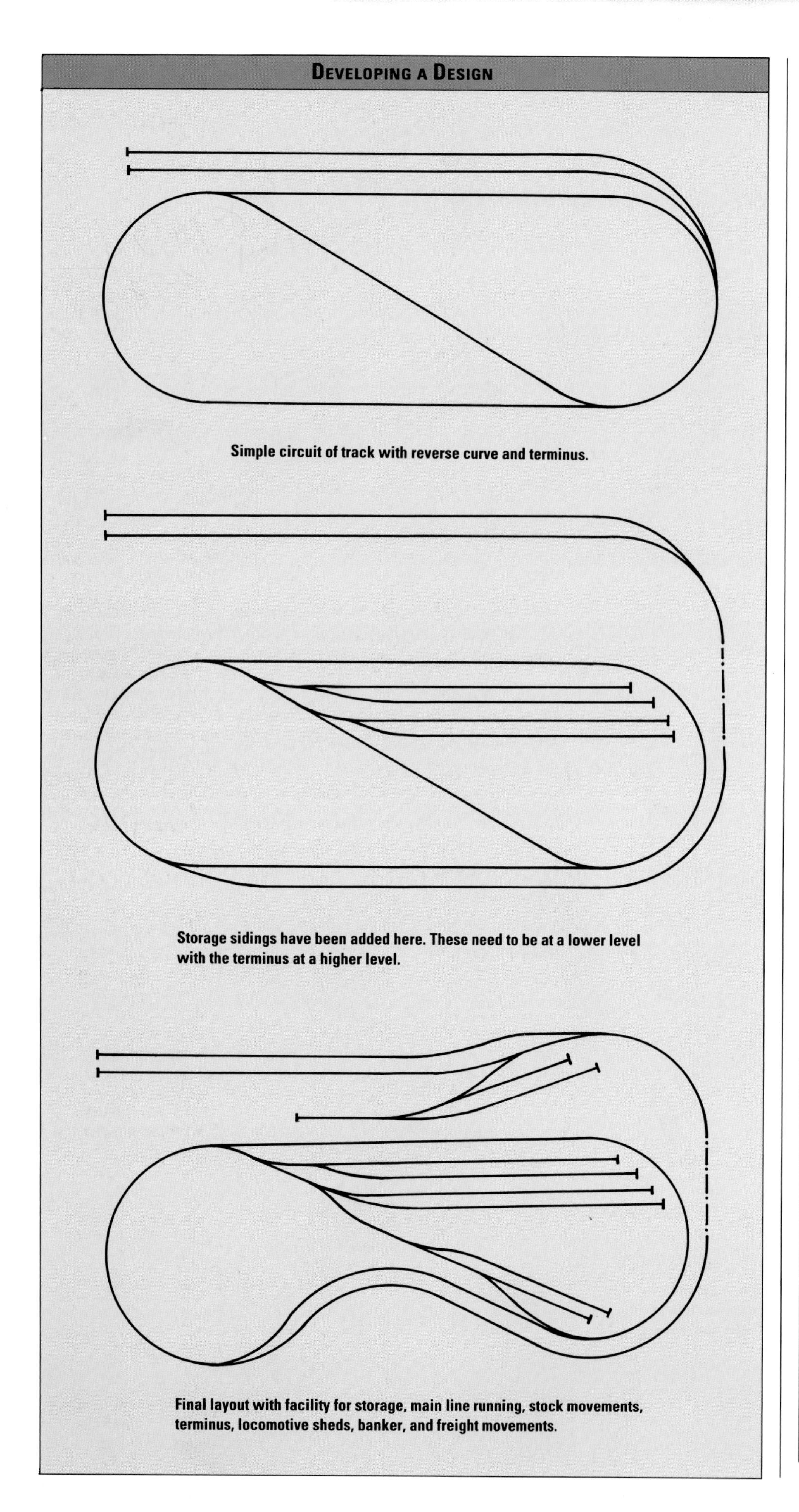

Simple circuit of track with reverse curve and terminus.

Storage sidings have been added here. These need to be at a lower level with the terminus at a higher level.

Final layout with facility for storage, main line running, stock movements, terminus, locomotive sheds, banker, and freight movements.

Several years ago I built a layout that I still really enjoy operating. It was built in a reasonable space of time (six months for the first section) and, most important, is still being added to. I have added both rolling stock and locomotives to replace aging items and to incorporate new classes, plus extra sections of base board.

My original idea was to have my own complete railroad system in model form. It is set at the turn of the century, in Victorian Britain, and built to the scale of 4 mm to 1 ft, and to S4 standards. It has a track gauge of 18.83 mm, which, when converted to full size, is 4 ft 8½ in – standard gauge.

While my initial layout of a small spur-line terminus was more akin to a diorama, it was built with a larger scheme in mind; it was to be just the first part of a theme that will eventually be expanded to include a port, a main line junction, gasworks, and engine shed for storing the locomotives that I build. To date, the spur line and port have been completed (pictures of them can be seen on page 16), the gasworks is under construction, and the engine shed is still at the planning stage. In a few more years I might have finished these parts of my layout, but, then again, a layout is never really finished – like all rail systems, things can be added, changed, or improved.

The biggest mistake a layout designer can make is to take a board and then design a layout to fit it. It is best to design the layout *first* and organize the woodwork to fit it. This way, only minimal changes to the design will be required.

### HELPFUL HINTS

When designing a layout, draw your plan first and then build the base to fit – do not try to make your design fit into a small space.

Make your layout operational – you will get bored with just watching your rolling stock go round and round on a simple circuit.

Choose a scale that will suit the space you have available to build your layout in. N-gauge takes up half the room of HO/OO.

A layout is never completed, so always allow room for expansion.

Start small and expand a little at a time, but keep your overall plan in mind at all times.

**ABOVE**

This very impressive station building is to 7 mm scale and measures 4 ft (1.2 m) long. Not only are all the exterior features faithfully reproduced from kits, but each building has complete interior details, including working lights.

**LEFT**

This impressive stone quarry, complete with crushing plant and loading buildings, is entirely operated by freight engines and trains – not many passengers here – but tremendous potential for enjoyment operating the various trains.

**ABOVE**

Diagram of the diorama which is illustrated on this page. Some parts are completed, but space has been reserved on the left side for further additions. The numbered arrows show the positions from which the photographs were taken.

**ABOVE**

The left-hand side of this diorama, which only measures 4 ft (1.25 m) across, has a rural engine shed complete with water tower. The detail is superb – even the fact that excess water would run into a cut and make an ideal habitat for ferns has been incorporated. This model shows that a layout does not have to be all trains to be interesting. A tremendous amount of detail can be worked into a small model such as this.

**LEFT**

This scene is a British Victorian sea front. Over a hundred little figures are used here, each repainted appropriately for the scene. This was the first extension to the layout and took about three months to build. Even though it is small, it is highly detailed to create a sense of realism. Operational considerations were also very important in this part of the layout.

**ABOVE**

Here is the other half of the diorama. It contains a small branch terminus and spartan freight and sidings. It is set at the turn of the century, so the milkmaid is driving the cows into the pens ready to be collected and taken to market. Each shingle of the station's roof is glued in place individually to create the effect of tile slates lying on battens very realistically.

Before starting to draw, list the requirements of the layout you want to build, trying to think of as many things as possible. Here are some suggestions for a basic layout with a degree of scope:

- main line running – single circuit
- terminus station – with return loop
- to accommodate a number of fixed trains – storage sidings
- each train to have two engines – plenty of locomotive movement and shed space
- main controller and switch controller – independent of each other, allowing two trains to move at once.

Using these headings as parameters, I designed the layout. Expanding on the main points further, the implications, in terms of both the type of stock it can carry and its potential operation, can be seen as follows. Starting with the terminus, I decided that an engine and three cars was a reasonable length train to be accommodated by the platform. Also, there had to be enough room for the second engine that would bring the train into the terminus and would then be uncoupled and isolated.

Having determined the size of the terminus, I decided to give it an impressive overall roof. This can look very attractive and distinctive. It will be features such as this that will give your layout originality and individuality.

One of the worst things about train sets is the sharp radius curves, but these are a necessary evil as gentler curves would make the layouts too big. These curves need to be very seriously considered. Somehow they have to be disguised, leaving only the straight sections showing. To do this, I decided to create a town at the terminus station end and, at the other end, a mountain or hill to cover the two tracks. Also, incorporating a reverse curve (the diagonal in the diagram on page 14) means that when the engine is run around the reverse loop, it will be facing the other way, so it turns it around.

Wanting to run a number of different trains means that they need to be stored somewhere when they are not in use. I accommodated this need by creating a series of storage sidings under the main terminus on a lower level, which meant I needed a two-level layout (see the diagram on page 14). Also, a cut is needed to provide a way of getting the trains from the lower-level circuit and storage sidings up to the terminus. In fact, *two* areas are required: one on the lower level which will accommodate a holding siding where engines are put once they have been turned and wait until they can go "light engine" back to the main shed on the upper level. The final plan is shown on page 14.

**ABOVE**

**Putting road and rail together always creates a lively combination and never more so than at a switchyard. The small space holds a variety of features, both architectural and mechanical, and a great deal of attention has been paid to detail and texture.**

Finally, always try to keep the main track circuits accessible so that the layout can be extended at a later stage.

The planning stage of any layout project is, therefore, very important, and a great deal of thought needs to go into it. Including as much detail as possible on the plan – even down to the routes the wires will take to the electric plugs, where the controller will go, and where the switches and turnout levers are to be situated – avoids many unnecessary problems and a great deal of frustration later on.

705
2001
WESTERN PACIFIC

2

# SOLID FOUNDATIONS – BASES

**LEFT**
**A finished layout based on an open-framed board. Here is an imaginative use of this construction technique, showing a scene of tracks running on two levels.**

The most fundamental element of any model railroad, no matter what size, is a suitable base board; a firm base on which to create your masterpiece. Good choices are plywood, blockboard, or hobby board. This last option is available from most specialist model railroad suppliers and is the ideal choice. It is lighter than blockboard, but needs more softwood cross-braces to prevent the sagging of long lengths, which results in undulating tracks. Whichever of these materials you choose, it must be soft enough to tap in the tacks easily.

A board base is a necessity for a model railroad if locomotives and stock are to be kept clean, well maintained, and, particularly, free from fluff. Fluff, by accumulating in engine mechanisms, causes clogging of the wheels, gears, and axles and removes the oil which is so important to their smooth running. A permanent base, usually consisting of a softwood framework with a suitable covering, keeps everything off the floor and provides a stable environment. It also makes it possible to store track easily and take layouts to exhibitions.

Storage is all-important. The nature of model railroads means that they tend to take up a great deal of space. So, if you do not have the luxury of a large attic or workroom, once you have finished with it, a base board can be stored away. For example, it can be fitted with castors and rolled under a bed, designed to be folded up against a wall, or even slung from the ceiling by means of pulleys and ropes, so that it can be pulled up out of the way when not in use – most ingenious.

In this chapter there are step-by-step instructions for constructing a simple base on a frame of 1 × 2 in (5 × 2.5 cm) softwood. This frame is then used as the basis for an open-framed base (see the top diagram on page 21). For the purposes of illustration only, a 2-ft (60-cm) square section of board has been constructed. Simply lengthen the side pieces for the standard sizes of boards, such as 4 × 6 ft (1.8 × 1.2 m), even 4 × 8 ft (2.4 × 1.2 m) or whatever other size you want.

For layouts where greater height, width, and depth are required – a mountain range or a deep valley or canyon scene, for example – then greater use should be made of plywood as, although heavier than hobby board, it will be easier to achieve a level surface. The photographs of completed scenes show how such humble beginnings can be the basis for stunning models when taken a stage further on a bigger scale.

For fully landscaped open-framed bases, the cross-bracing can take the form of plywood profiles. The landscape must be accurately planned beforehand, but this

**ABOVE**

**In this beautifully detailed layout, using the open-framed baseboard technique, the track in the foreground is running down an incline which, further on, loops around to pass back and under the bridge.**

**LEFT**

**Here the open-framed base technique is used to create the lovely feature of a road viaduct passing over a railroad running along a cut.**

## Basic and Open-framed Base Construction

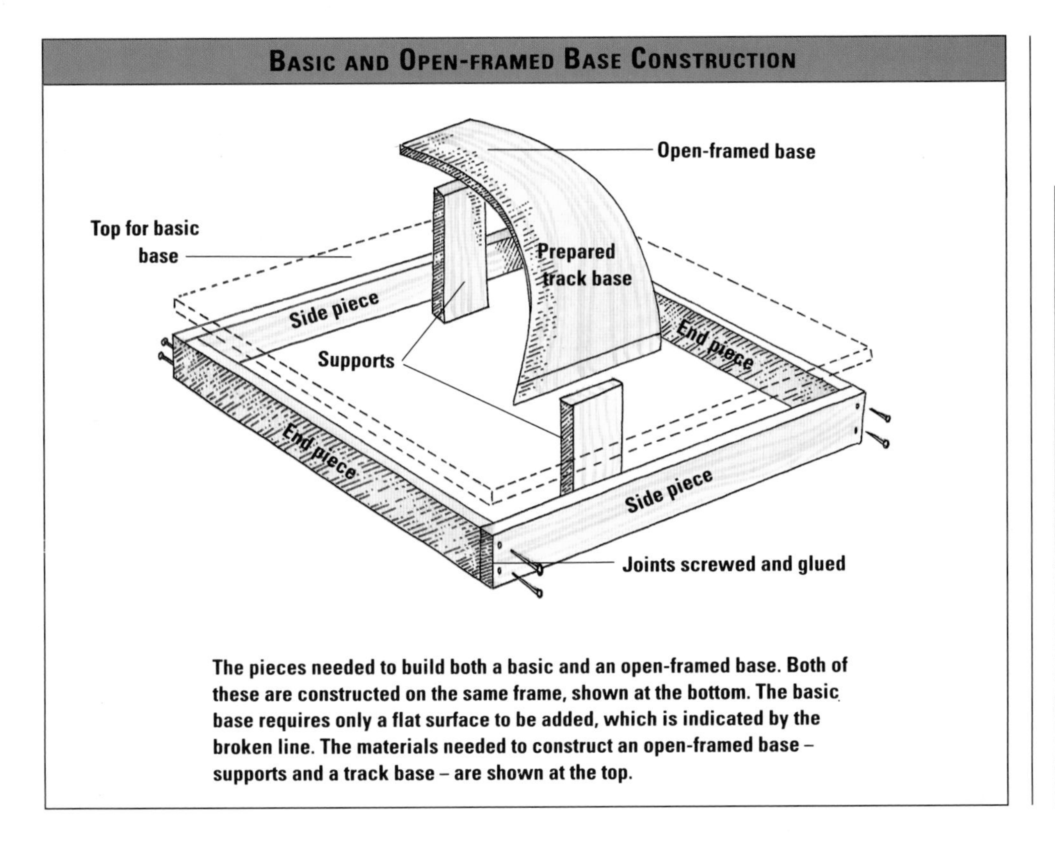


**The pieces needed to build both a basic and an open-framed base. Both of these are constructed on the same frame, shown at the bottom. The basic base requires only a flat surface to be added, which is indicated by the broken line. The materials needed to construct an open-framed base – supports and a track base – are shown at the top.**

### HELPFUL HINTS

Use a suitably sturdy material for the base surface and make sure that it is well supported.

Measure the required piece of wood several times and then cut once – this eliminates many mistakes.

Choose the best type of base construction to suit your project – if you want to create really mountainous scenery, for example, you will need to build an open-framed base and add extra height using plywood formers.

Always use a carpenter's square to mark measurements and cut on the outside of the pencil line.

When choosing softwood, go to a lumber yard where you can see if it is straight.

can be done easily if, at the end of the design stage, a small-scale model (say a scale of 10:1) is built from cardboard and balsa strips to prove the design. The completed model can then be used as a visual check during all stages of the construction of the real thing.

When joining sections of plywood, always add fillets of wood of about 1 in (2.5 cm) square, making sure that they are well glued and pinned, for secure joints. Each stage of construction requires 24 hours of drying time, having made sure that the joints are square and even before leaving them to dry, as it will be impossible to adjust them once the glue has set.

It is essential during construction to make good use of various clamps, in particular the very useful corner clamp. Because of the good strength-to-weight ratio of this form of construction, it is possible to lighten the structure by cutting holes in the cross-braces. Also light diagonal cross-bracing can be added to strengthen the structure, making triangular shapes where possible, as these are strongest and most resistant to twisting.

## Creating Extra Height on an Open-framed Base

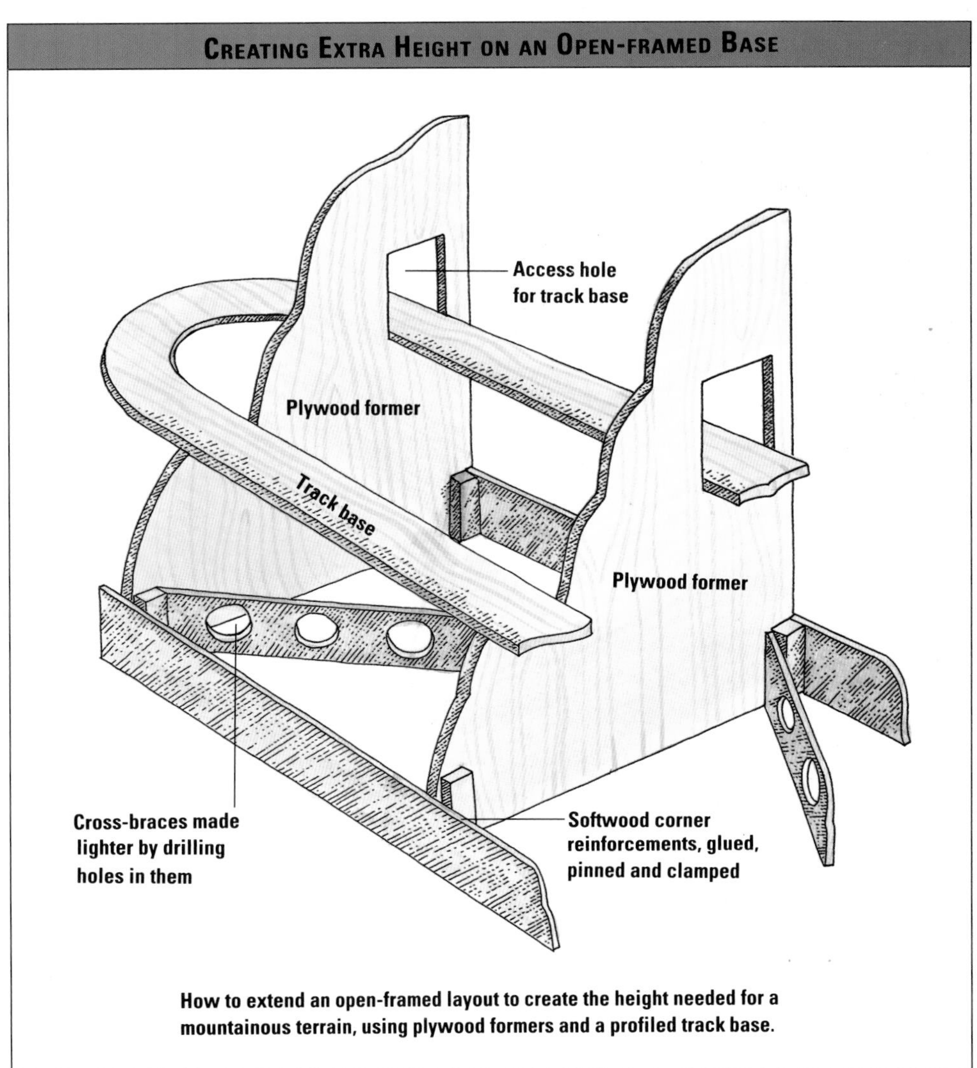


**How to extend an open-framed layout to create the height needed for a mountainous terrain, using plywood formers and a profiled track base.**

# BASIC BASE

1 *Here are the tools and materials needed to complete a basic base. They include a work-bench (or suitable other clamping base); power drill, saw and screwdriver, or manual equivalents; tape measure; pencil; carpenter's square; screws; wood glue.*

2 *Using the tape measure, the required lengths of wood are marked with a pencil. You need to have two end pieces and two side pieces cut to the dimensions to make the size of base you require.*

3 *Aligning the carpenter's square carefully with the marks, a clear line is drawn across the wood, and a mark made to indicate on which side of the line to cut.*

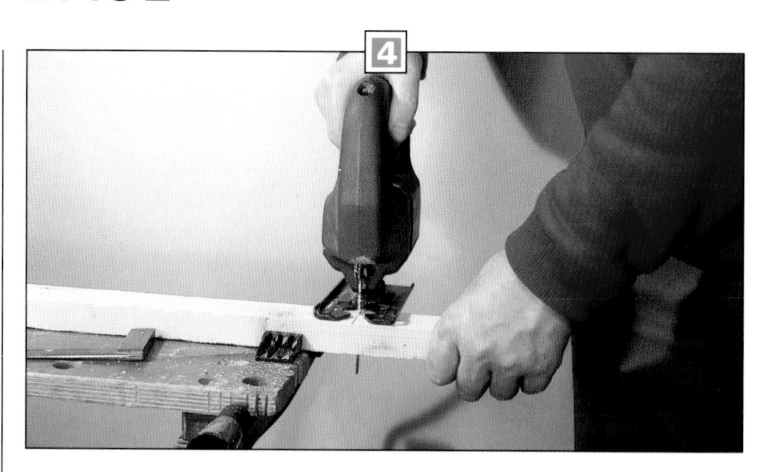

4 *When cutting, the cut should be made along the outer side of the measured mark so the resultant piece of wood is the correct length.*

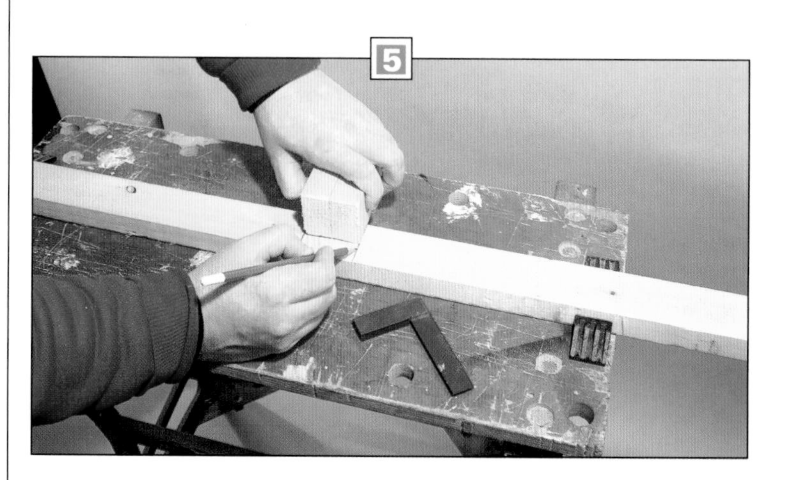

5 *The two end pieces fit inside the sides in order to form a square, so they need to be shorter than the sides by two thicknesses of wood.*

6 *Here are the four pieces of the square. The ends are aligned to show how the two side pieces are shorter by two thicknesses of wood (see the spare pieces of wood resting on top).*

7 *The holes are pre-drilled in the end pieces, which will be screwed and glued to the side pieces.*

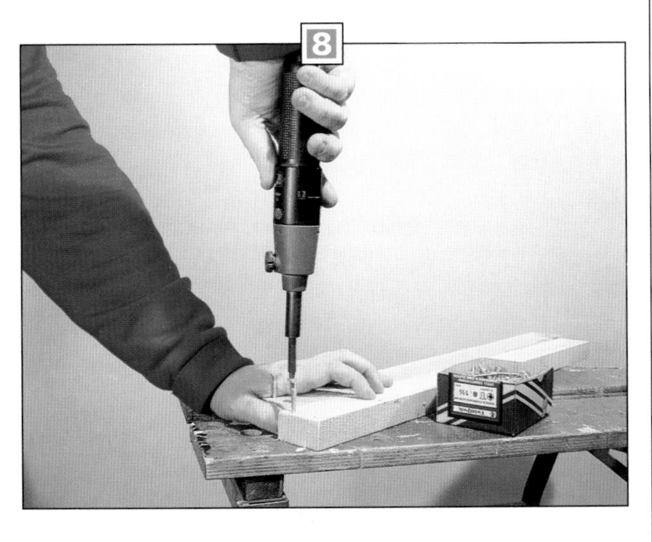

8 *Once the holes have been drilled, the screws are partially screwed in so that their tips are flush with the back.*

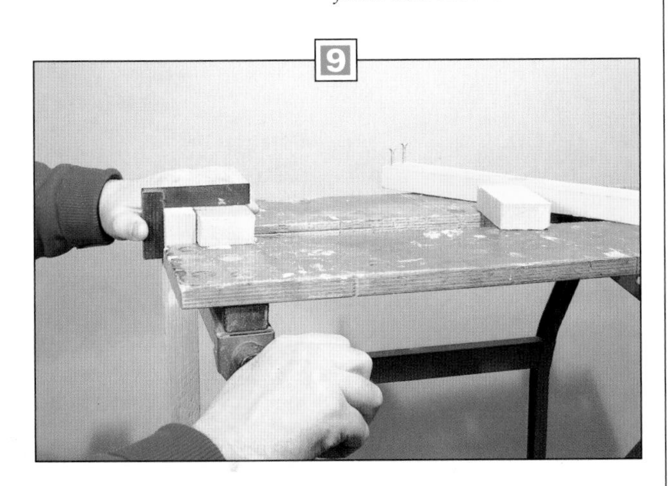

9 *Using a suitable clamp, one end of a side piece is inserted so it is proud of the top by a thickness of wood (measured using a scrap of wood).*

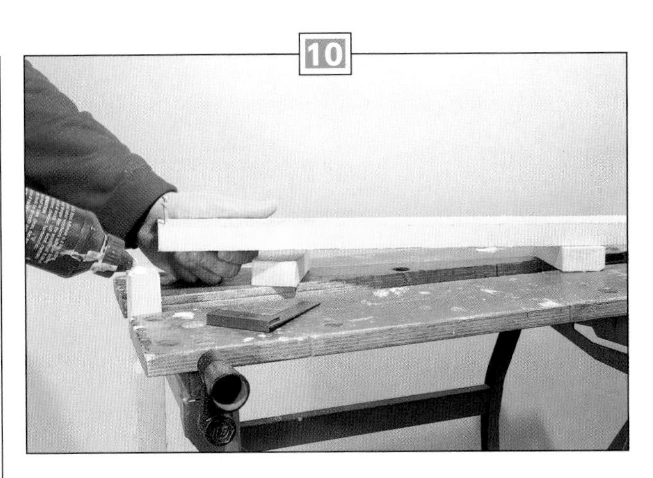

10 *Wood glue is applied to the end of the clamped side piece, and the prepared end piece is placed on it, aligning all the edges squarely.*

11 *Resting the other end of the end piece on a scrap of wood so that it is level, the screws are tightened into the side piece.*

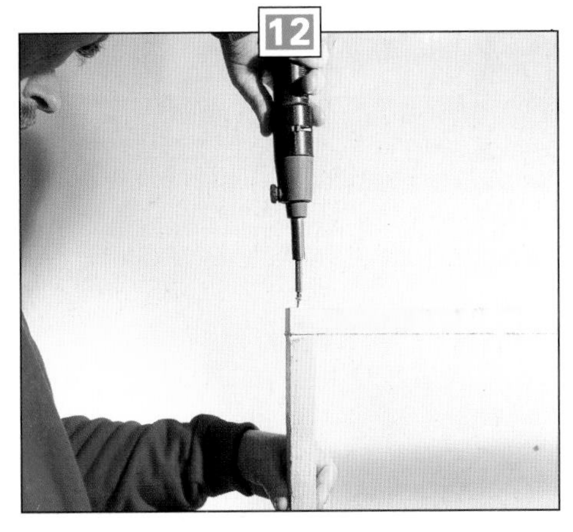

12 *This process is repeated for the other end of the end piece, forming a U-shape; then the other side piece is added in the same way to complete the square.*

13 *There are a number of materials available that modelers can use to make base tops. From the top down: hobby board, block-board, and plywood. These simply need to be cut to size.*

14 *Wood glue is applied to the edges of the softwood frame. Holes are drilled in the board at equal intervals, placing them half the width of the edge of the frame in from the edge of the board.*

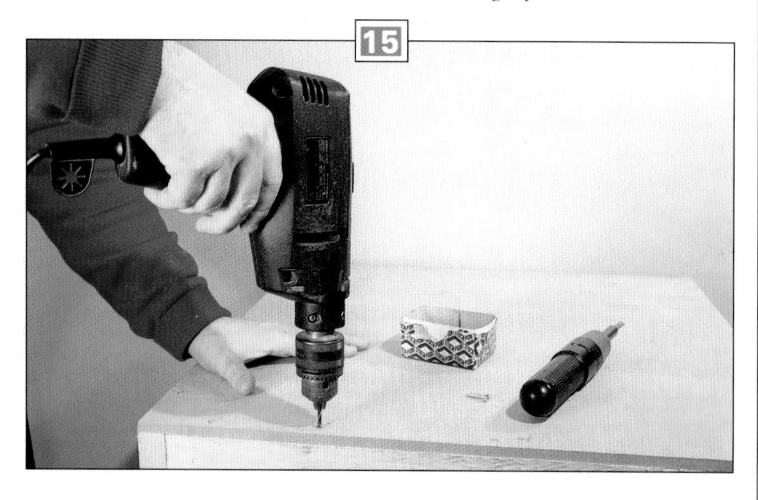

15 *The board is laid on top of the glued frame, aligning the edges carefully. The board is screwed to the frame, feeding the screws into the pre-drilled holes.*

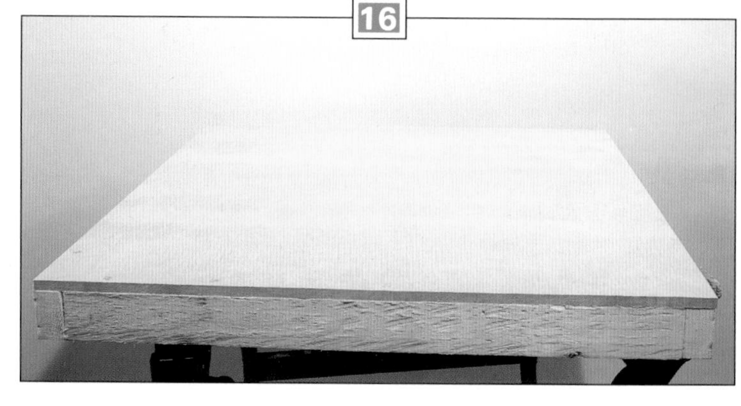

16 *The finished base after being left to dry for 24 hours.*

17 *A suitable material for the surface of a base is one that will allow small track nails to be easily tapped into it to secure the track.*

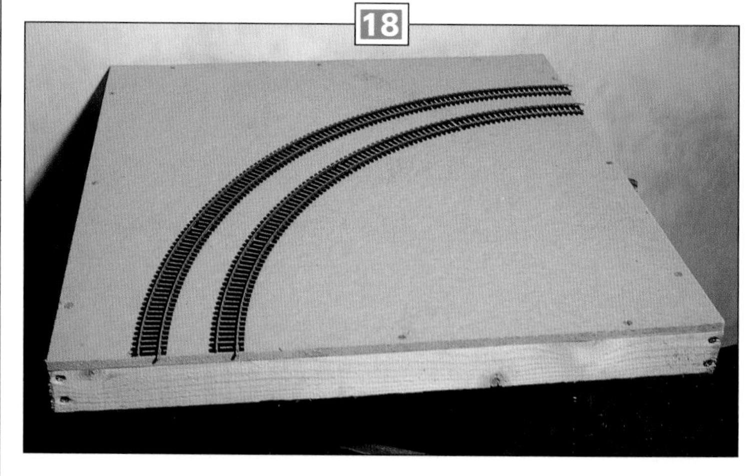

18 *Purely for demonstration we have constructed a simple 2-ft (60-cm) square board with a double track curve as the center subject.*

# OPEN-FRAMED BASE

1

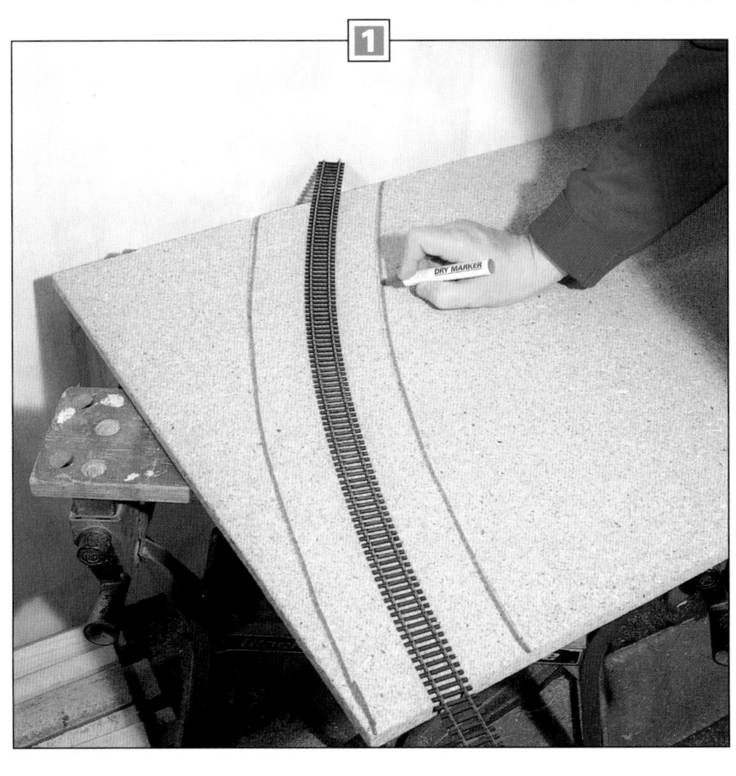


1 *The profile of the proposed track is marked (giving it a wide margin on each side to accommodate scenery later) on a suitably strong material, such as plywood, hobby board, or blockboard.*

2

2 *It is cut out, sawing along the lines, then attached to a softwood frame in exactly the same way as the basic base.*

3

3 *A second level can be added, which is secured to supports attached to the frame.*

4

4 *The height of the second level can be set as desired by altering the length of the supports.*

P M & GD
23

3

# SCENIC BASES

**LEFT**
**Impressive stonework forms an excellent backdrop to this layout, giving it both height and depth.**

This is the point at which only your imagination can limit what can be achieved. Indeed, inspiration is at the heart of many of the fine layouts illustrated in this book. From simple, plain fields to rolling hills or even floor-to-ceiling mountains, any topology can be achieved. The wide choice of materials available will enable you to create wonderfully lifelike scenes.

The open-framed base, as was seen in the last chapter, lends itself particularly well to the creation of scenery. As its name implies, the starting point is a basic frame. Two methods of filling the gaps in the frame are covered in this chapter. First, styrofoam blocks are suitably carved and shaped, then coated in plaster. The second method is best suited to filling bigger areas, where a lightweight filling is required, and uses wire mesh covered with plaster of Paris.

Always use a thick sheet of styrofoam, as used in the construction industry for insulating houses ~ the shapes used in packaging electrical equipment and so on are not suitable. The type of styrofoam used in packaging is not of a consistent density or thickness and creates more problems than it solves. For the purpose of showing both the styrofoam and the wire-mesh-and-plaster methods, the demonstration layout is split in half ~ one half built up using the first technique, the other half using the second.

# STYROFOAM AND PLASTER SCENIC BASE

1 Starting in the bottom corner, the first piece of sheet styrofoam is roughly cut out to fit onto the framework, but is not glued into place yet.

2 The next layer is cut and shaped, including tapering the face nearest the track base a little using an old bread knife.

3 To simulate a rock face, which will form one side of the cut for the lower track, cork bark (available from florists) is used.

4 The styrofoam layers are cut away enough to take the thickness of the cork bark.

5 *As noted earlier, the track base needs to be wide in order to accommodate the rock face as well as the track.*

6 *The final layers of styrofoam are added, again profiling them to shape. When the shape is as desired, the styrofoam layers are glued together using suitable cement and then left for several days, preferably in a warm place, to cure.*

7 *Once the base has set solid, a thin layer of instant plaster is carefully applied to the surface of the styrofoam. This is then left to cure.*

# CHICKEN WIRE AND PLASTER SCENIC BASE

1

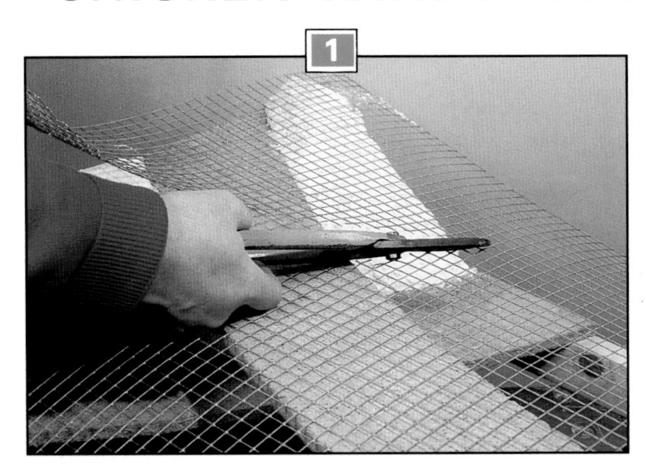

1 *A piece of chicken wire that is roughly the same size as the gap to be covered is secured underneath the top track base using a staple gun.*

2

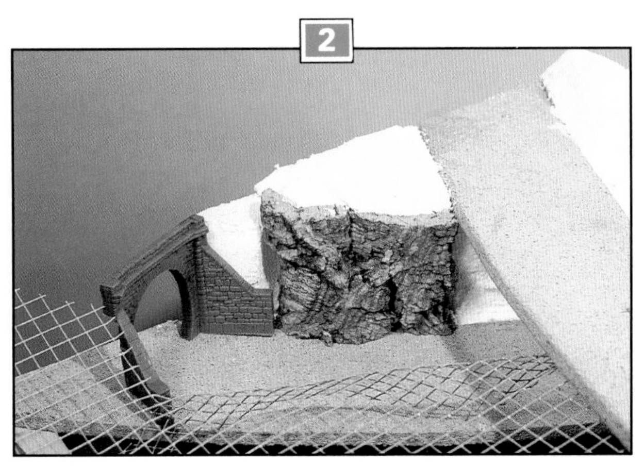

2 *It is carefully bent over and down to meet the lower track base and trimmed as necessary, and the plastic tunnel mouth is put into position.*

3

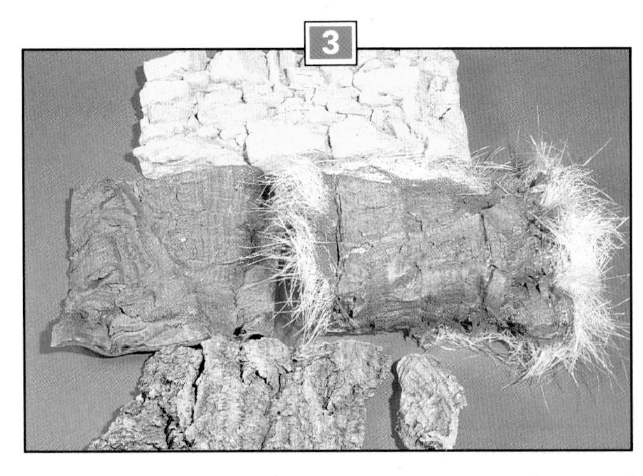

3 *Rock textures come in various shapes and sizes. Here, from top to bottom, are resin casting and fiberglass molding (front and back) made from a sample of bark, such as that at the bottom.*

4

4 *Here the rock face is being built up with pieces of cork bark, blending them into the base with plaster mix.*

5

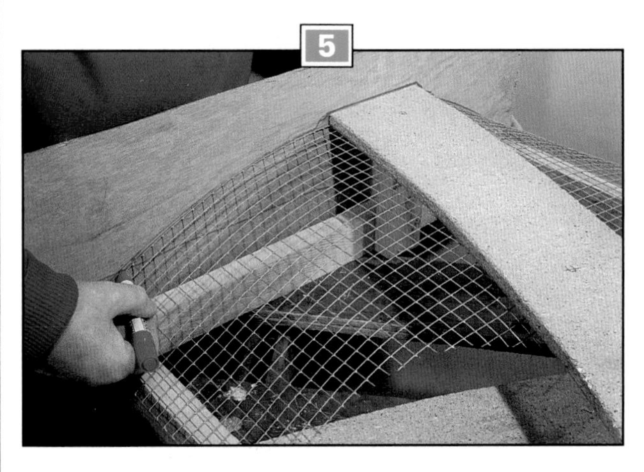

5 *Using the wire as a guide, a piece of plywood is clamped to the frame and the proposed profile drawn onto it.*

6

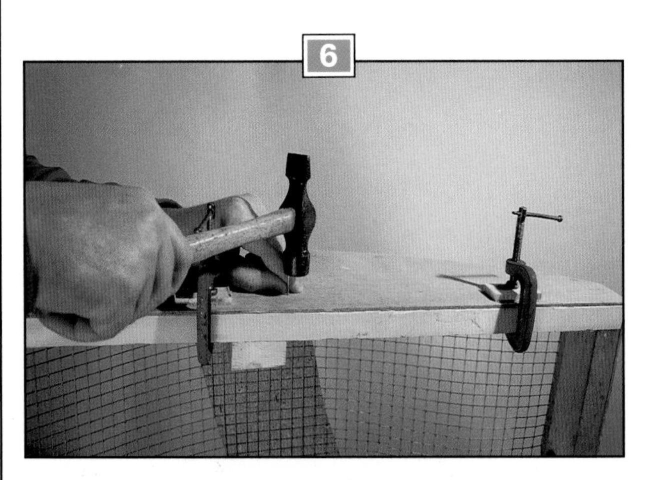

6 *The plywood is cut out along the profile, then this shape is glued to the frame. The plywood profile is clamped in position and secured to the frame with brads.*

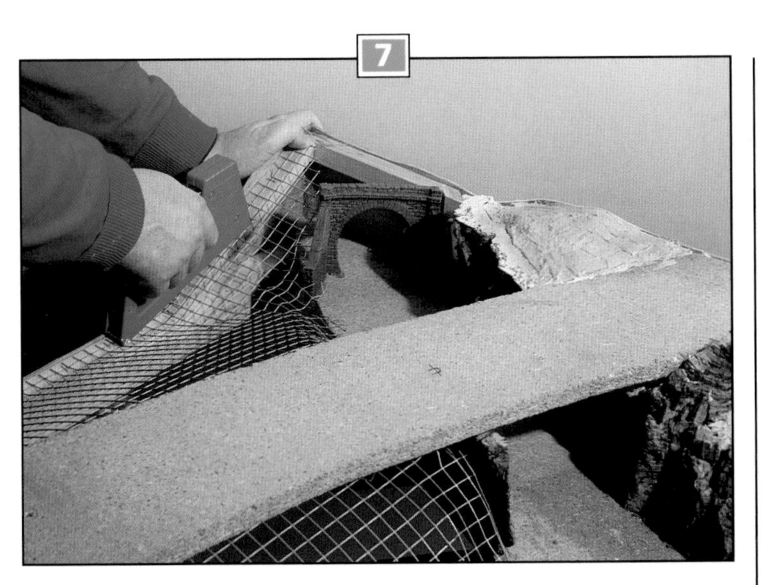

7 *With the profiled sides in place, the remaining chicken wire can be stapled to the frame. Where necessary some 1 × 1-in (2.5 × 2.5-cm) battens are glued to the inside faces of the plywood profile to provide anchor points for the wire.*

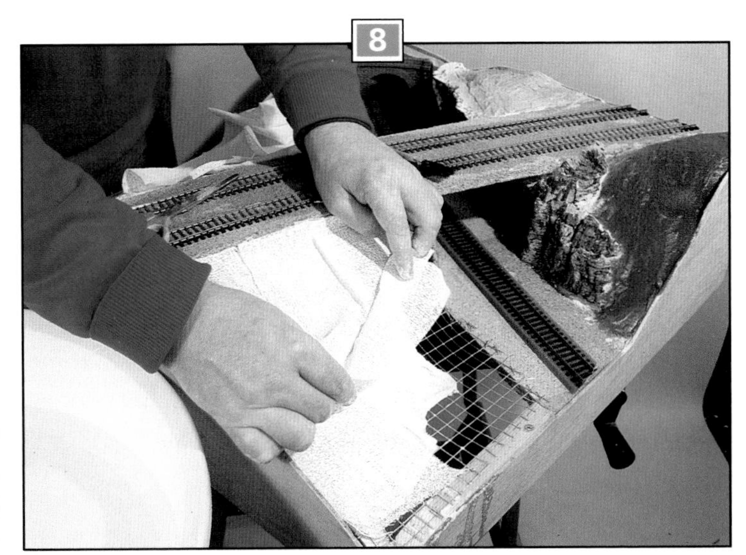

8 *Then strips of bandage soaked in plaster of Paris are laid over the chicken wire frame. It needs to be pressed down well around the edges, or it may peel away later. The track ballasting shown here is described on page 39.*

9 *Once all the mesh has been completely covered, the layout has to be left to dry out and set solid. The finished result is a strong, but reasonably lightweight scenic base.*

# HOW TO MAKE REALISTIC ROCKS

**BELOW**

**This multilevel layout, easily achieved using an open-framed base, has been imaginatively constructed. Here, the track in the foreground passes under the track above. A plastic tunnel mouth, when suitably painted with various stones picked out in different colors, is very effective.**

This can be achieved in many different ways, and it may not be the obvious technique that will produce the required effect. One of the simplest ways to create a rock face starts with a trip to the local florist and the question, "Have you any cork bark?" Simply choose a piece that most closely matches what you want, but it need not be exactly right as it can be cut, filed, or even broken up into various other shapes or sizes as necessary.

After the basic scenic base has been laid in, select the area where the rock face is to go and choose a piece of cork that fits this space. Cut away the scenic base to accommodate the cork – any gaps can be filled in later with plaster or lichen (see step-by-step sequence, page 28).

Always keep an open mind when looking at any material. Rocks do not have to be the basis for rocks – they are often simply too big to use anyway. A material that has produced some very successful results is coal or ballast. Choose lumps that have the right sort of texture and shape, make a mold from them, and then they can be used again and again, producing a good supply of scenic rock material. This is how it is done.

Select half a dozen or so likely pieces and using a stiff-bristled brush, remove any loose pieces and dust. Spray a silicone-based furniture polish over the surfaces to prevent the mold from sticking. Paint the prepared

ABOVE

**This N-gauge European mountain scene displays some excellent effects, both in the use of rocks and in the bridges that link the trackwork across the open-framed base.**

coal with rubber solution glue and, while it is wet, lay strips of open-weave fabric, such as cheesecloth, that have been painted with glue, over the coal or ballast. Follow this with a second liberal coating of the glue. Next, lay more fabric strips over the glue, this time at right angles to those of the first layer, and give it a third coating of the glue. Leave it to dry. When it has completely set, carefully peel the mold away from the coal.

Other materials suitable for the strips are casement cloth, plaster scrim, gauze, or any other material that is thin and becomes very limp when it is wet so it can be pushed around the shapes well, producing an accurate mold.

The rubber solution glue, when applied the first time, lies thickly on the horizontal surfaces but tends to slide off the angled and vertical surfaces, so when adding the fabric strips, paint them on both sides with plenty of glue for these areas. Make sure, too, that the strips follow the contours well, fitting snugly into all the depressions.

Watch out for air bubbles under the cloth, which will spoil the effect. Cut the material into 2-in (50-cm) wide strips and when laying them over the coal, slightly overlap them. Make sure that each strip is thoroughly wetted with the glue and all of it is in contact with the coal before applying the second layer of strips. The second layer is placed at right angles to the first to produce a tough mold that is unlikely to split.

You can tell when the mold is dry because the glue changes color from a snowy whiteness to a translucent, "rubber band" hue. How long the mold will take to dry depends on temperature, humidity, and the amount of air movement there is, but during the summer, leaving it overnight will be sufficient.

Now to producing plaster rocks. Obviously rocks made entirely from plaster and used in large quantities on a layout will make it heavy, so it is best to use a combination of fabric and plaster of Paris to achieve a light but strong construction. Gauze bandage can be used instead of

**RIGHT**

**The corner of a stone quarry here is, in fact, not very deep, but the relief modeling and painting is so true to life and so perfectly matched to the scale of the rolling stock that it is extremely convincing.**

### HELPFUL HINTS

A staple gun or a hot glue gun are both ideal for securing chicken wire to a wood framework.

When using plaster bandages, lay down the strips carefully, but make sure they combine with each layer.

When sticking styrofoam together, use the correct glue or disaster will result.

Always blend rock representations into the base with a plaster mix – do not leave unsightly gaps underneath the rocks.

Take extreme care when shaping or carving styrofoam blocks to form the basic structure of hills and valleys.

**RIGHT**

**These rocks were produced using a mold taken from a piece of coal, and they work very well.**

cheesecloth. Lay the molds open side up and cut strips of bandage that are 1 in (2.5 cm) wide and just long enough to line the molds. Mix a plaster slurry by adding enough plaster to a bowl of water to give a fairly sloppy mix – not too stiff, or it will dry too quickly. Pour some into the mold and push it and roll it around so that all the inside surface of the mold is covered with a thin layer of plaster. Then, dip the bandage strips in the remaining plaster and lay them in the mold. This has to be done quickly as the plaster starts to set in about three minutes.

After five minutes, it is quite safe to pull the plaster rock gently from its mold. Every minute feature of the lump will be reproduced, but it will not be heavy. The casts can then be cut to the required shape and it is also possible to crack the casting by bending it. The bandage strips will prevent the parts from separating completely, giving the cracks a very natural appearance.

It is possible to reproduce quite effective rock faces by spreading thicker plaster onto a surface and then shaping the plaster with knife and spatula, but the rubber mold and casting method is easier and usually more realistic. It is also very quick. Although it may take an evening to produce a selection of molds, the next day a production line is soon operating, with rocks being ready to pull from their molds every few minutes. It is also possible to alter the shape of the rocks in terms of flatness or curvature as required by the layout. Because the molds are rubber, they can simply be bent to various shapes and held there during the few minutes of setting time. In this way, odd-shaped rocks can be produced to fit the most awkward spot and also the rocks themselves can be cracked and bent, so a "Grand Canyon" can be yours by next week if you so choose.

**BELOW**

**Good use of a high rock face made from shaped plaster gives a realistic backdrop to this American N-gauge layout.**

2431
L N W R
L N

# ADDING COLOR

**LEFT**

**The stone wall in this layout threads its way across rolling green hills. On close examination, it is clear that realistic grass is made up of a variety of colors.**

Having made a good base and added the basic scenery it is now time to start adding color and make the layout generally more realistic.

Powder paints are ideal for painting the rock faces shown in the last chapter. Painting very watery reddish brown color on first and adding extra washes one after another builds the color up gradually and it can be altered as you go rather than finding that the initial color is too intense for the effect you want. Using more dilute black or green washes in places helps to make things realistic. It sounds a most slap-dash way of going about things, but amazingly, the best results are achieved by slopping liberal quantities of the paint on to the plaster and letting it run where it wants. In some places it puddles on a horizontal surface and gives intense color, while other areas remain only slightly tinted. A useful tip for green or black paint is to put paint on a small brush and apply it to one spot, allowing it to trickle from the brush, resulting in an uneven line of color. This then represents an area where a slight trickle of water has encouraged the growth of moss and lichen. Such unevenness adds texture and a lifelike quality to the surface.

The two bases constructed in the previous chapters will now have color added in two completely different ways. The first method uses straightforward scenic mats and the second uses paints and flocks on the plaster base. Nearly the same effect can be achieved using either technique. Scenic mats are the simplest thing to use, but on a plaster base you have the option of adding a wider range of delicate colors ~ so you can create any landscape you like.

# SCENIC MATS

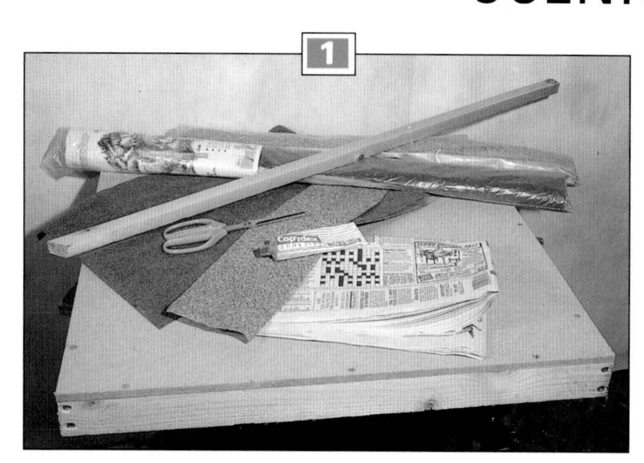

1 *The simplest scenic material to use is a scenic mat. These are widely available in different shades and textures.*

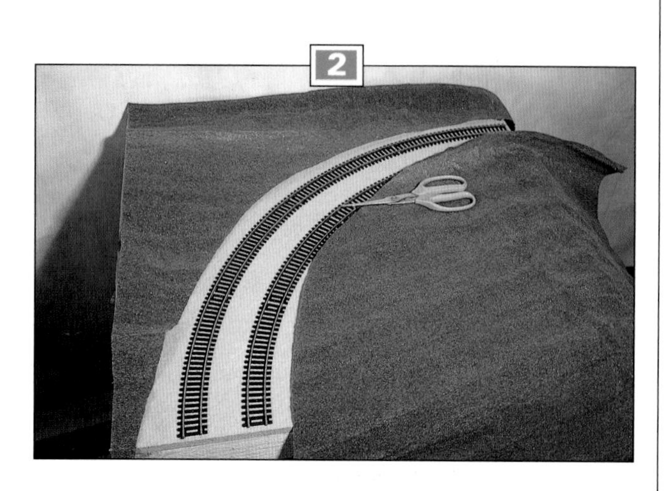

2 *The scenic mat is cut out so that it is roughly the shape of the board or, as here, the area to be covered on each side of the tracks.*

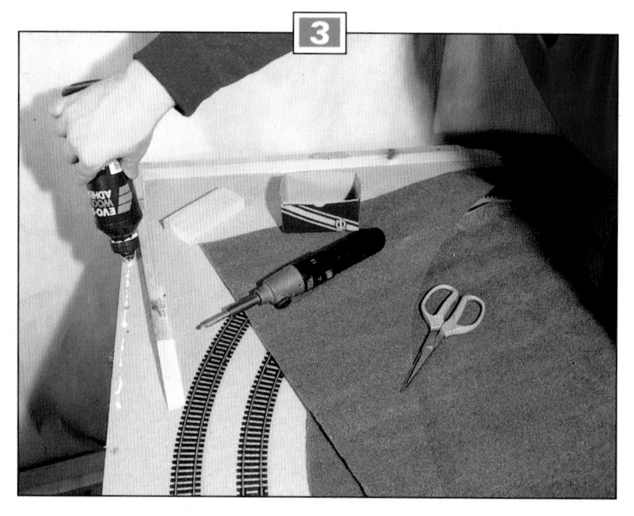

3 *In order to give the scenic mat realistic form, 1 × 1-in (2.5 × 2.5-cm) battens are glued and screwed to the outer edges of the board.*

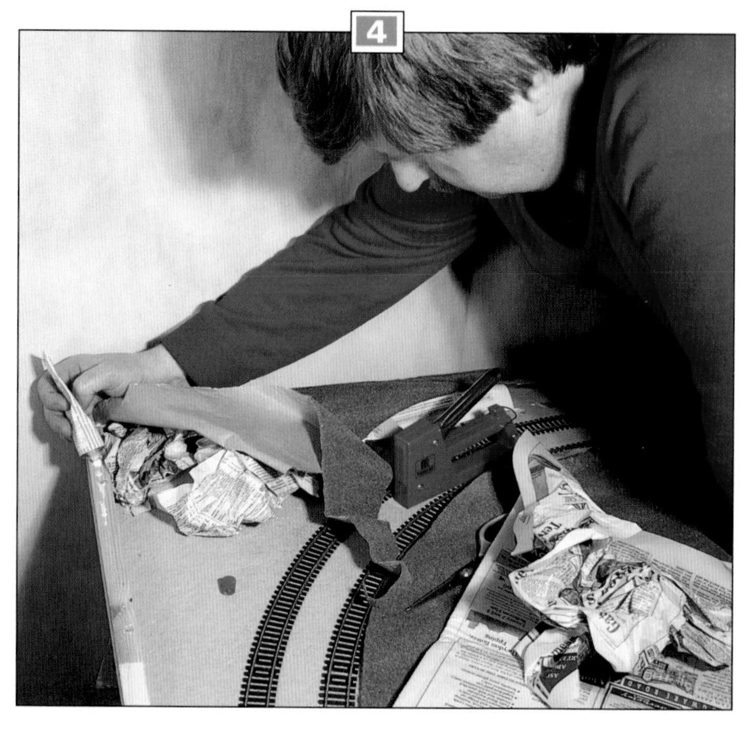

4 *The edges of the scenic mat are stuck to the battens at one corner using rubber solution glue and left to dry. Then some crumpled newspaper is carefully pushed under the mat. The edges of the mat continue to be glued down as the desired shape is built up.*

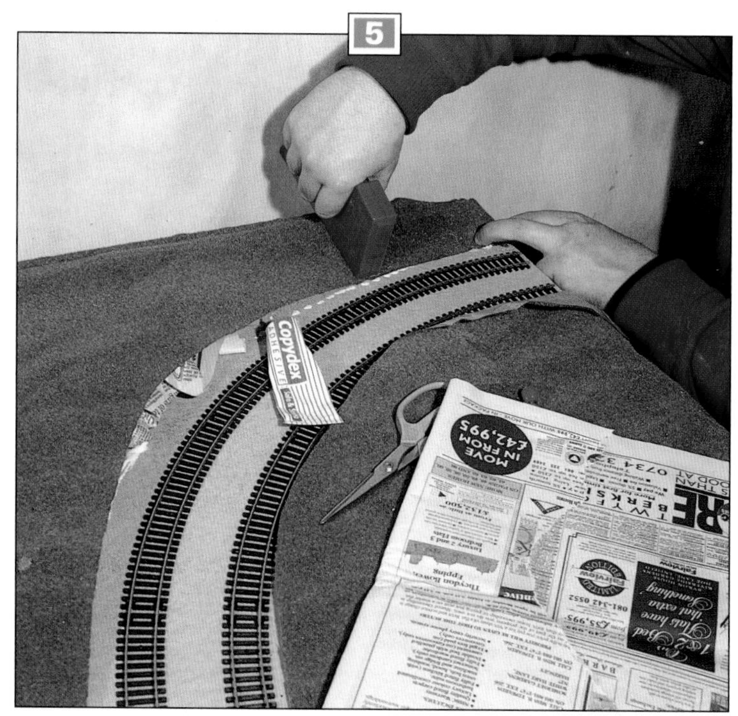

5 *When the right shape has been produced, the edge of the mat close to the track can be glued and stapled into place.*

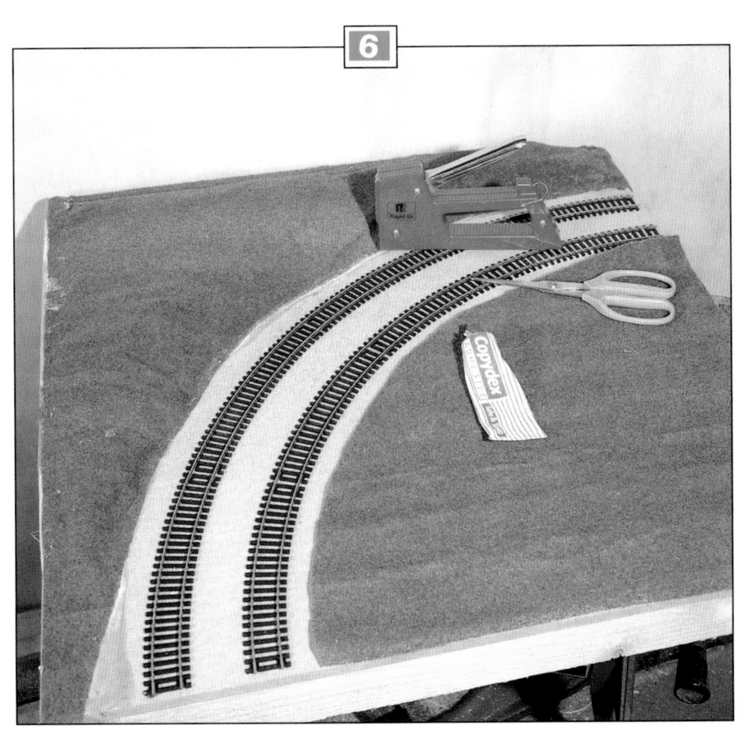

6 *Already, with just this basic addition of color and form, a simple train set starts to become a model railroad.*

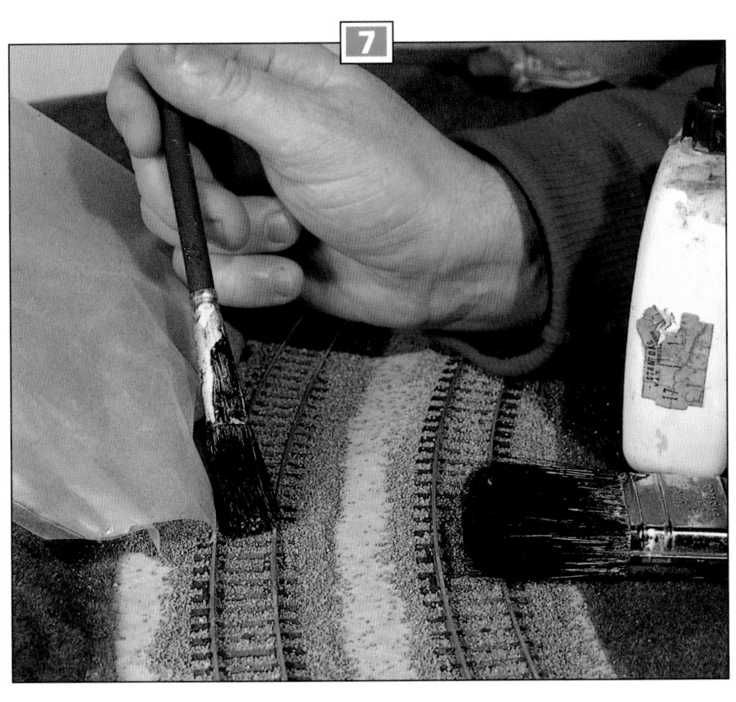

7 *Next comes the ballasting of the double track. Initially the ballast material is poured along the tracks and spread evenly with a brush, leaving a gap between the two tracks and at the ends.*

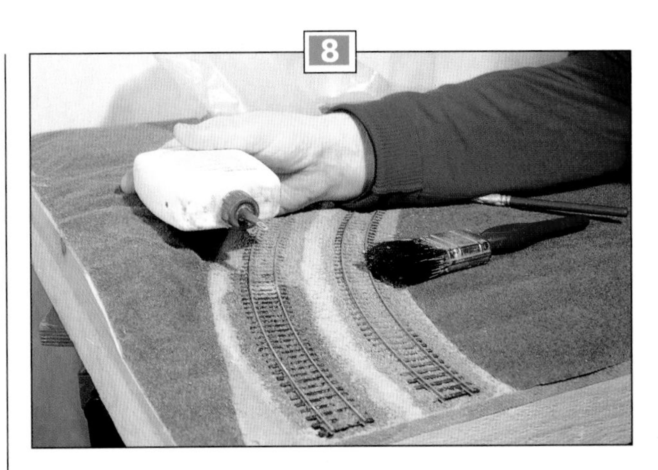

8 *A mixture of half wood glue and half water, together with a few drops of dishwashing liquid, is poured evenly over the ballast to hold it in place.*

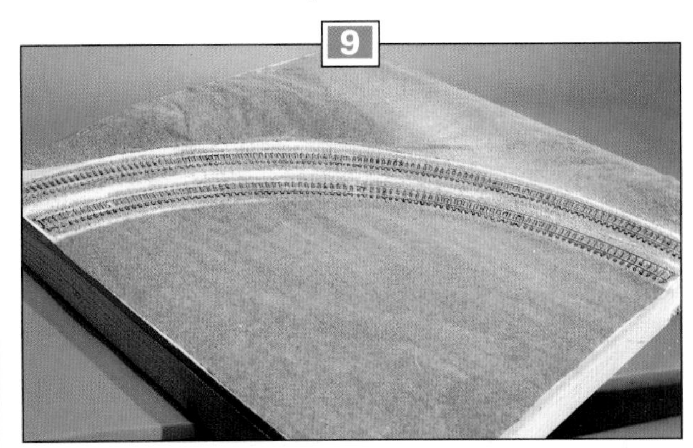

9 *The basic display has now progressed dramatically from being simply a board with tracks pinned to it.*

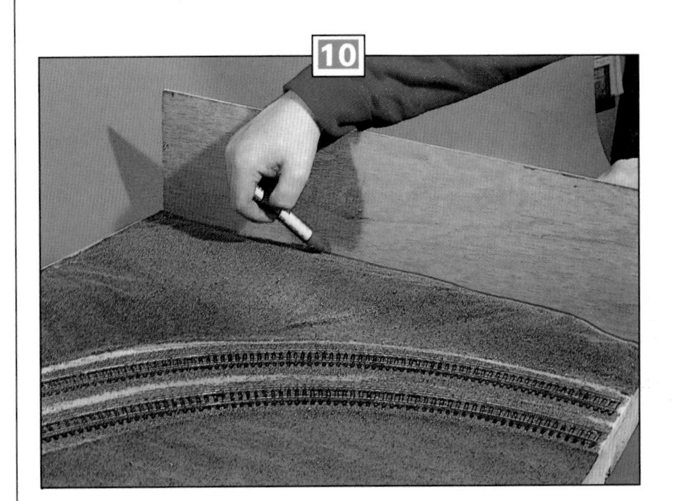

10 *To finish the edges, some thin plywood sheets cut out to the profile of the edges of the base are added. These are simply glued and nailed to each side as before. They can then be painted or stained as appropriate.*

# COLORED FLOCK

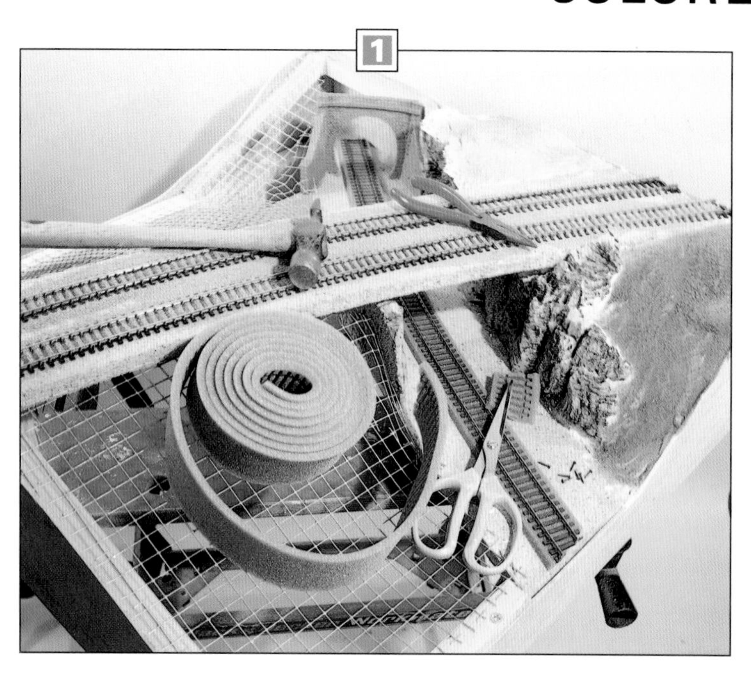

1 *For the open-framed layout, an alternative technique for ballasting is shown on the lower track. This makes use of commercial foam underlay, which speeds up laying time and has the added advantage of quietening the running of trains. To ballast the track using foam, simply place a strip of foam underneath the track and hold it in position as the track is tacked down.*

2 *At the end of the last chapter, a white plaster scenic base had been produced. The first job, therefore, is to tame the white, and here green spray paint has been used as a base. Any styrofoam has to be coated with plaster before using this, however, or the paint will dissolve it – that is, unless you want caves!*

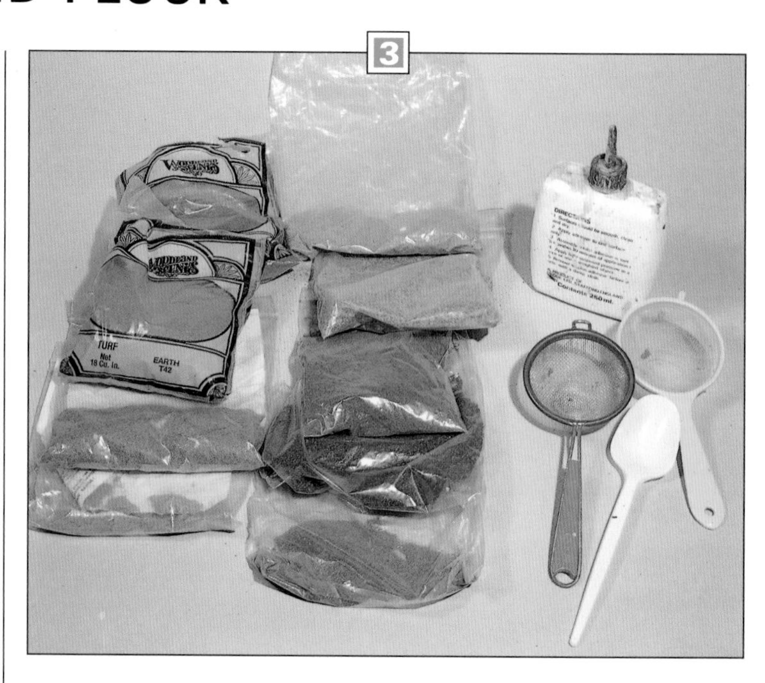


3 *Analyze any scene from nature, and it is soon clear that it consists of an incredibly wide range of hues and colors. Thus, a good selection of variously colored flocks are needed. The small strainers and wood glue and water mixture (see page 39) are for applying them.*

4 *The area to be colored is painted liberally with the glue and water mixture.*

5 *One strainer is filled with a couple of coarse flocks to form a good base that soaks up the glue mixture when subsequent layers are added. The other contains highlight colors – a mixture of several of these produces the variations seen in nature.*

6 *The highlight colors are sifted over the base of coarse flocks once it has dried. To break up the lines of ballasting, a sandy brown colored flock is used. Secure the ballast as before (see page 39) with the glue and water mixture. Before it dries, take a spoonful of the flock, and tap it to scatter the flock along the strips, blending them in.*

7 *Similarly, where track has been laid on foam underlay, the areas between the tracks and the scenery need to be filled in. The technique used in the last step achieves this beautifully.*

8 *The large grassy area is treated in the same way as the slope around the rock face, using a mixture of greens.*

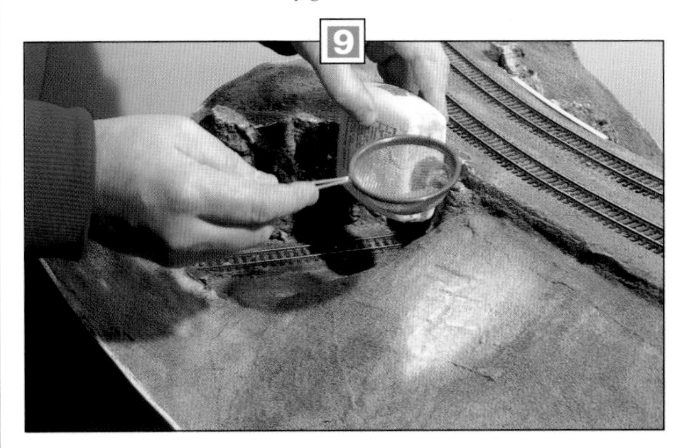

9 *Adding second and third coats of flock to the grassy area builds up the texture. Each layer begins with the area being coated with the glue and water mixture.*

# FINISHING ROCKY AREAS

1 *In order to complete the rocky area on the opposite side of the track to the rock face, pieces of cork bark are broken and glued to the surface with wood glue. The joins between the rocks and the ground are covered by building up layers of the flock material until they blend together.*

2 *The single biggest improvement that can be made to commercial track after it has been laid and ballasted is to paint the sides of the unnaturally shiny rails a much more believable rusty color. This is a fairly time-consuming and fiddly task, but the end result is well worth it. A piece of N-gauge platform edging has been glued on. The abrasive block shown in the picture is used to clean paint and glue from the tops of the rails.*

**RIGHT**

**Nothing looks more impressive than a long, sweeping curve with a colorful train threading its way through the open countryside – especially when the landscape has been recreated as sensitively as it has here.**

LEFT

**The steep hill has been built using the chicken-wire-and-plaster-bandages method described earlier, providing a colorful backdrop for this country terminus. Note the clever variations of color and texture, so reminiscent of the real thing.**

HELPFUL HINTS

Do not make scenery unnecessarily complicated if a simple option will give the same effect.

When simulating green grass, study nature closely, and you will see that it is made up of a combination of many colors.

Build up ground coverings with several applications of flock ground powders, liberally adding glue each time.

Add several drops of dishwashing liquid to the basic 50/50 mixture of glue and water used for fixing ballast, as this will allow the glue to spread easily.

Tone down the shiny sides of new rails by painting them a realistic, rusty color.

RIGHT

**This rural spur line runs along the top of an embankment, allowing plenty of scope for modeling bridges and roads.**

# ADDING GROUND-LEVEL FOLIAGE AND TREES

1 *Ground-level foliage is made by teasing and cutting a suitable piece of lichen into the correct shape and gluing it in place. All kinds of trees are available, and "planting" them is straightforward. Simply make a hole slightly smaller than the diameter of the tree trunk, dab some glue onto the end of the tree trunk, and push it into the hole.*

2 *The board has been divided into two different landscapes to show a variety of scenery. This side has rolling green fields and deciduous trees, which have been added here in the same way as the pines on the other side.*

3 *Here is the finished scenic base, with basic plant and landscape features in place. The next step is to add the scenic details.*

4 *Even before further details are added, just putting some stock on the tracks means that this is already an enjoyable little railroad.*

**RIGHT**

Having a purpose is all important, and this point is clearly demonstrated by this scene from Dr. Charles Patti's Wingfoot and Western railroad, which features a shay-geared locomotive pushing a gondola under the tipper.

**BELOW**

The trackwork here is on one level, while a river and gently sloping embankments have been built up to meet it, forming a very pleasing scene.

"CANADA DRY"
The Champagne of Ginger Ales
PM&GD 28
RR
28

# SCENIC DETAILS

**LEFT**
**The foreground rockwork has been carefully blended into a painted backdrop that makes the overall view more convincing. Note, too, how well the curve at the end of the layout has been disguised with trees and how lichen has been used to simulate scrubby bushes.**

Once a good scenic base has been achieved, adding the scenic details really brings the layout to life. More important, this is one area of modeling where you can really go to town ~ working solely from your imagination or drawing inspiration from everyday life. Take a trip into a small town or the countryside with a notebook and camera (preferably with color film) and record what you see. Note how farm animals congregate in fields, see how buildings are grouped together, and notice the different architectural designs. Also look at aging and weathering, so that, when you come to reproduce your version of the real thing, it will be authentic in both structure and texture. This does not only apply to buildings; it is applicable to everything including road vehicles, signs, hedges, fences, and trees ~ all of which have their own ways of aging. In this chapter are some good examples of such details, plus some cameo scenes. Follow the simple step-by-step instructions for the techniques you need to produce marvelous detailing.

# HEDGES AND WALLS

*These things look unlikely sources of scenic detailing material but are, in fact, excellent. You will already know how good cork bark is for representing rocks, and lichen for ground-level foliage and so on, but what about the broom and the pan scourer? Read on.*

## LICHEN HEDGES

*Lichen is the easiest material to use. To make hedges, suitable pieces are simply cut and shaped as required, then a ribbon of wood glue is spread along where the hedge is to go and the prepared lichen pressed into the glue.*

## FLINT STONE WALLS

1

*... walls, the pan scourer is ... ut 1/4 in (5 mm) wide, ... he longest side.*

2

2 *In an old dish, wood glue and water are mixed in equal quantities. Then, holding the clips attached to the ends of each strip, the strips are pulled through the glue mixture.*

3 *Some of the granite ballast is spread out on a piece of paper and the glue-soaked strips are gently rolled in it and then hung up to dry. A second coating of glue and ballast is sometimes needed to cover the scourer completely.*

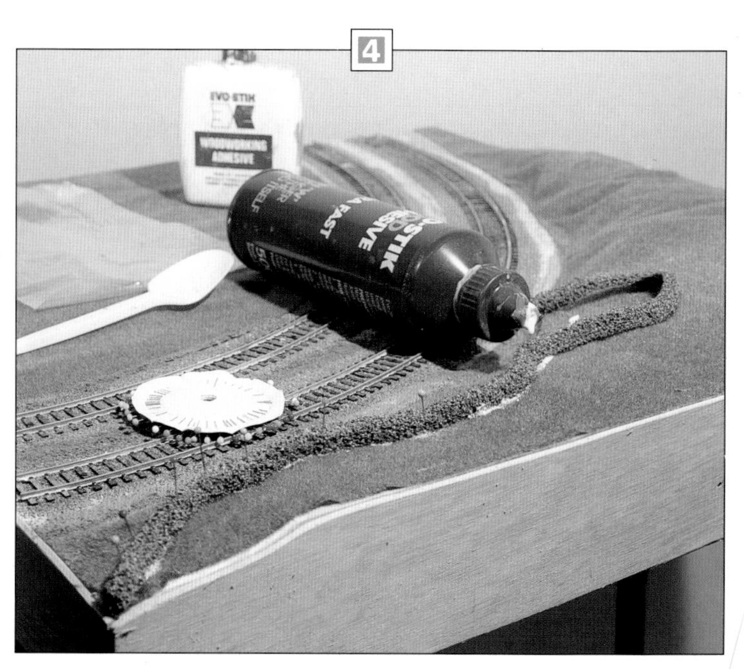


4 *The finished wall is glued in place. A few long pins inserted at intervals keep the wall upright while the glue is drying.*

5 *Once the glue has dried, the pins are pulled out of the wall. The lichen hedge can be added while the glue is drying. Here the hedge is being alternated with the wall to break up the scene.*

# WHEATFIELD AND ROOT CROPS

## WHEATFIELD

1 *How about adding a wheatfield? This lifelike impression took two weeks to create, but the effect makes it all worthwhile.*

2 *How was it done? Imagine that the green material is the part of the scenic base where the field is to go. Some wood glue is spread over the area and, when the glue is sticky, the bristles of the broom are pressed into the glue and the broom is supported to keep it straight. It is left for at least 24 hours to dry thoroughly. When it is dry, the bristles can be cut to whatever height is needed. An area about 2 in (5 cm) square can be done at a time, slowly building up the field to the required size.*

### HELPFUL HINTS

Look for everyday items that can be used to represent real things in miniature – like the bristles from a broom which can be used for a field of wheat.

When adding livestock to fields, observe how sheep and cows group themselves at different times of the day.

Use a variety of materials for railroad perimeters. Fencing, hedges, trees, or walls can all be used to make your layout more interesting.

Use the right glues for the right job – wood, plastic, and metal materials all have their relevant adhesives.

## ROOT CROPS

1 *Rows of root crops always add interest to a country scene and are easy to make.*

2 *Some finely corrugated cardboard is colored to match the earth of the surrounding area. The color of the earth varies in different parts of the world – here the cardboard has been left its original color. Lines of glue are drawn along the "peaks" of the corrugations.*

3 *Some flock in an appropriate grade and color is spread onto a piece of paper, then the cardboard is carefully and gently pressed onto the flock. When it is lifted, any excess is tapped off. It is left to dry and then can be trimmed and glued into place in the field on the scenic base.*

WATERWITCH

# WATER FEATURES

**LEFT**
**This period diorama of Exbridge Quay features some excellent, fully detailed sailing ships floating on real water.**

Water does contribute greatly to making any layout really eye-catching. Even from the earliest days of the railroad, there has always been a strong connection between rail and canals and rivers. Competition between the two modes of transportation certainly caused conflict, but it was the natural courses of the waterways that the major railroads used as a guide when building their lines. Next time you are out, see how many times railroads and waterways are interconnected.

While water features on layouts are generally created from casting resin or plastic sheets, for which there will be step-by-step instructions later, we start with the real thing. Dave Rowe, who has created many superb working dioramas, where real water features have been incorporated, lets us in on several of his secret techniques.

# MAKING A POND

Freshwater ponds liven up otherwise bland areas of layouts. The step-by-step instructions are for two different techniques used to insert ponds in the basic layout produced in earlier chapters.

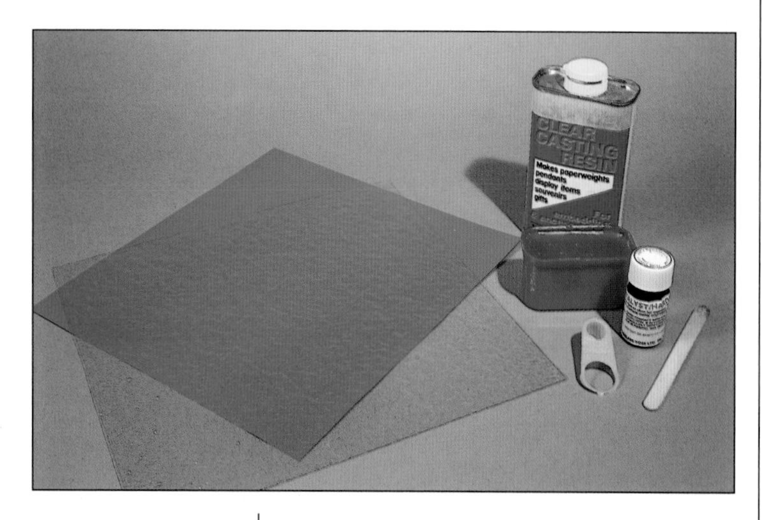


*The two techniques used to simulate water in this chapter require the materials shown here. Left is a sheet of rippled plastic and suitably colored paper, while on the right is clear casting resin, together with hardener and measuring and mixing equipment.*

### HELPFUL HINTS

When pouring resin to represent water, make sure the base is completely sealed.

Before the resin sets, you can add a few brush bristles to represent weeds or bulrushes.

If you use real water, make sure that it never comes into contact with any of the layout's electrics.

Clear glue can be used to simulate the odd puddle of water caught after a downpour of rain.

Try representing fish by using strips of foil in either resin water or real water.

## FIRST METHOD

1 *The base and scenic mat are cut out to the pond's shape.*

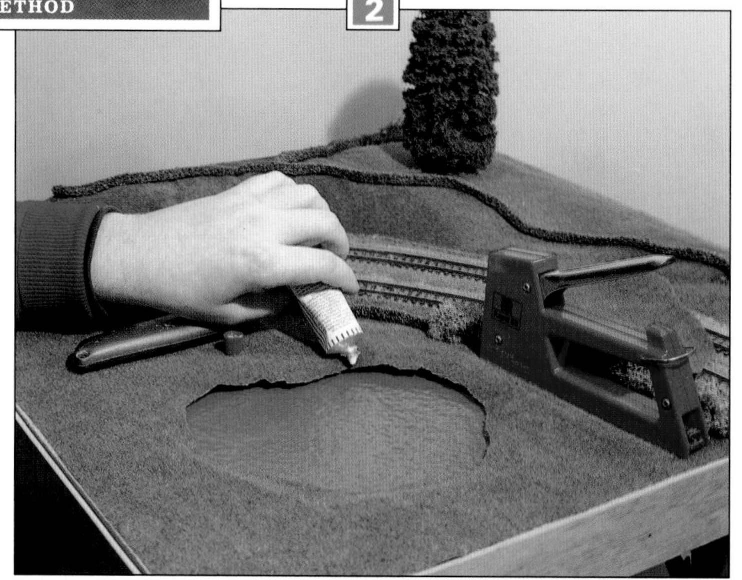

2 *The rippled plastic and paper are placed underneath the hole, and a staple gun is used to attach them to the back of the base. The edge of the scenic mat is then glued in place to the surface of the pond.*

## SECOND METHOD

1

1 *For a more realistic representation of a pond, a "sub-base" is made first. The pond area outline is drawn on a suitably sized spare piece of the base material, and then grit and flock are glued into place.*

2

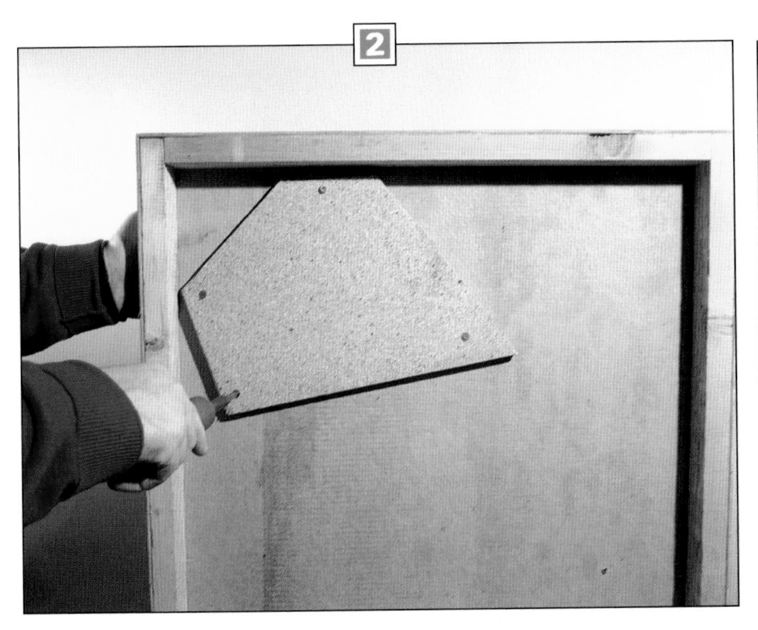

2 *The sub-base is then positioned underneath the hole for the pond in the base and screwed in place, first spreading some silicone sealant (such as that used around baths) around the margins of the pond sub-base to prevent the casting resin from escaping later.*

3

3 *The edges of the scenic mat are glued to the bottom of the pond and blended in with a layer of flock as necessary.*

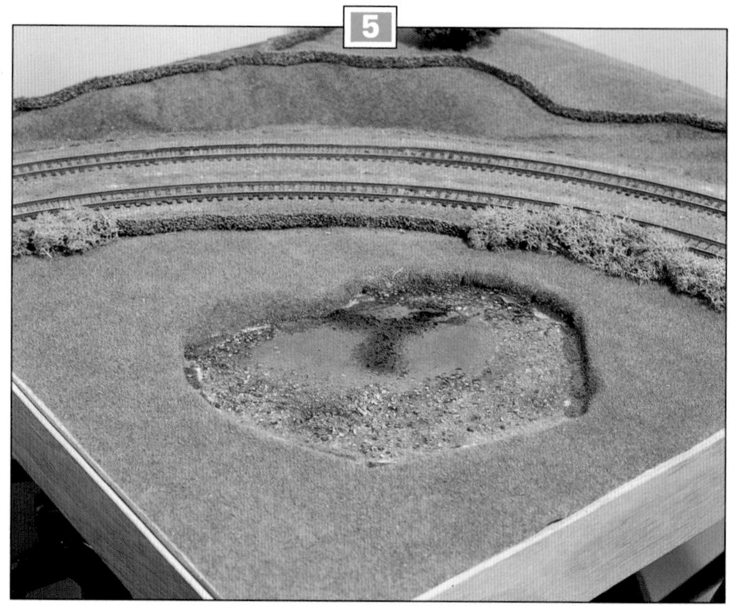

4 *The casting resin is made up according to the manufacturer's directions and left to stand for several minutes before being poured into the pond. It is carefully spread over the bottom of the pond until a good covering is achieved.*

5 *Several layers need to be added to produce the correct depth shown here, each layer being left to set before the next is added.*

**RIGHT**

**To achieve this wonderfully watery effect, clear polyester resin has been poured over a painted, sealed canal base and built up from several layers. The top layer was "dragged" while it was curing to produce the realistic rippled effect.**

RIGHT

This sea scene has a mainline running across a sea wall and the track supported by a wooden trestle.

LEFT

Casting resin used in this pond reflects the light and laps the sides quite convincingly.

ABOVE

Quietly rippling waters are achieved using casting resin.

# OTHER WATER EFFECTS

Now to some techniques that produce very effective representations of water – even of the sea.

Very convincing areas of sea can be modeled using the thick, textured coating used by painters to give texture to walls and ceilings. Because of its consistency, it holds its shape, standing proud of the base, just as well as it does when it hangs down from a ceiling. The added bonus is that, once it is dry, it becomes rock hard.

The required amount is mixed (follow the manufacturer's instructions) and spread in a layer about ¼ in (6 mm) thick over the area that is to become the sea. A trowel is ideal for doing the initial spreading. A number of different tools can be used for the next part of the process, but a 1½-in (4-cm) wide paintbrush is ideal. The brush is pushed into the textured coating and gently pulled through the mixture and up, in the direction the imaginary wind blowing at the time would be moving. This produces a wave, which should keep its shape. This process is continued across the "water" until the whole area is filled with waves. The waves should be made to a size that suits the scale of the model.

Coloring the "sea" once it has set is a matter of individual interpretation of the scene and personal observations of real sea. A choppy sea on a dull, early winter day will call for mixtures of flat medium green, sky blue, and gray colors. Of course, the tops of the bigger waves should be highlighted with dirty white to represent the foam of breaking waves. Gloss varnish can then be painted on to give the sea the sparkle and sheen that is seen on real seascapes.

**BELOW**
**This choppy winter sea scene has been created using the textured coating more often seen on walls and ceilings in houses.**

# A LOCK USING REAL WATER

Using real water on any layout will instantly make a model stand out from the others, but it is of paramount importance that the liquid be contained completely. There must be no seepage and definitely *no* possibility of it coming into contact with the electrics. Finding solutions to these extra design parameters can be tricky, but results are definitely worth the effort.

Dave Rowe constructed a working lock on his diorama of a sand excavation site. The boats simply rise and lower on the surface of the water as the water goes in and out of the lock. The principle behind its operation is simple, but very effective. First, though, the boats are constructed from plastic as usual, but inside each vessel is a rectangular buoyancy tank made from 5/32 in (0.4 mm) thick nickel silver sheet, to ensure that they are watertight and float when they are placed on the water.

The canal fills and empties automatically, but the system does not use valves or pumps. An old tin can and motor are all that is needed to form the basis for the system! The diagram shows how it works.

**ABOVE**
**The centerpiece of this unusual diorama by Dave Rowe is the working lock. The two canal barges actually move up and down in the lock when the water enters and exits.**

**RIGHT**
**A working lock system, using real water. The motor (A) from an old 78 rpm record player is geared down to revolve the shaft (B) once every 3 minutes. The can (C), is suspended from the arm (D) and always remains vertical as it can pivot at the bearing (E). The rubber tube (F) connects the can to the lock (G). When the can is lowered below lock level, the water flows into the can and when the can is raised again the water flows back into the lock.**

## A Working Lock System

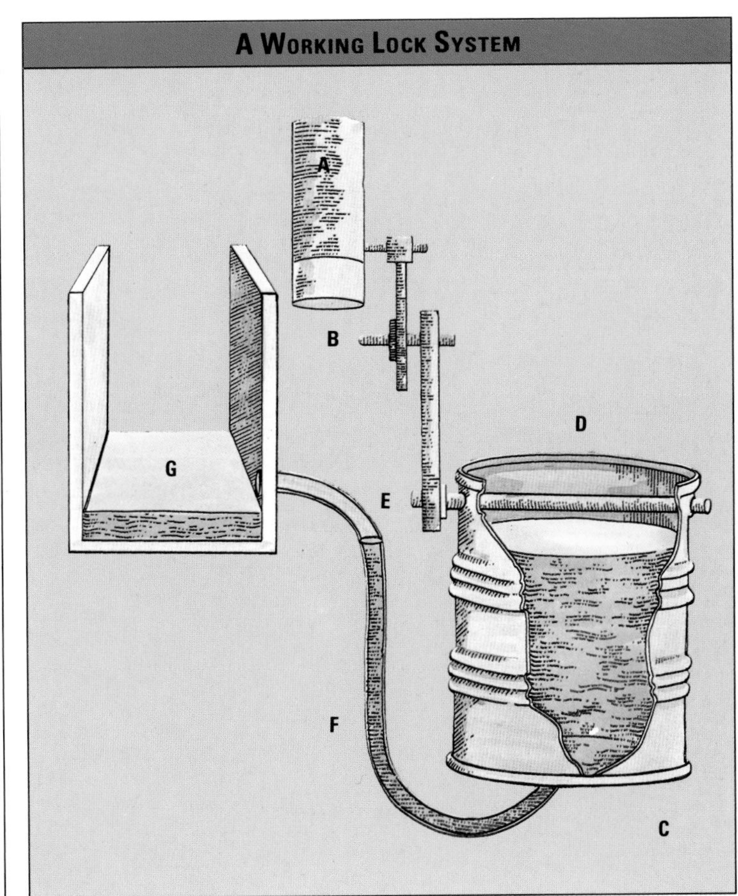

PLATFORM Nº 4
G
W
6415
SOUTHERN
RAILWAY
FIRST
BK-1829
GWR
FURNITURE REMOVAL
FROM HOUSE
TO HOUSE
SERVICE
ENQUIRE AT ANY STATION
39005
G
W
14098
G
PT WAY
Return to
Reading
W
20 Tons

# CONSTRUCTING PLASTIC KITS

**LEFT**

**Here is a scene of a freight yard that includes a large number of plastic freight cars conveying different loads. The detailing is of the highest standard.**

The first steps a modeler takes toward creating his or her own models rather than buying them ready-made, can take a number of different forms. The models can be simple buildings or cars for a freight train. The latter project is obviously the more interesting for a railroad enthusiast as you can create your very own train, which will actually move, and you can operate it knowing that you built it yourself! When starting out in your model railroad career, it is necessary to obtain ready-to-run stock to build up some reasonably long trains, but they will of course look a lot like those of other people. A move toward building your own rolling stock will give you a chance to create really individual models. It therefore seems appropriate here to start with a simple kit for a single domed tank car.

# PREPAINTED KIT

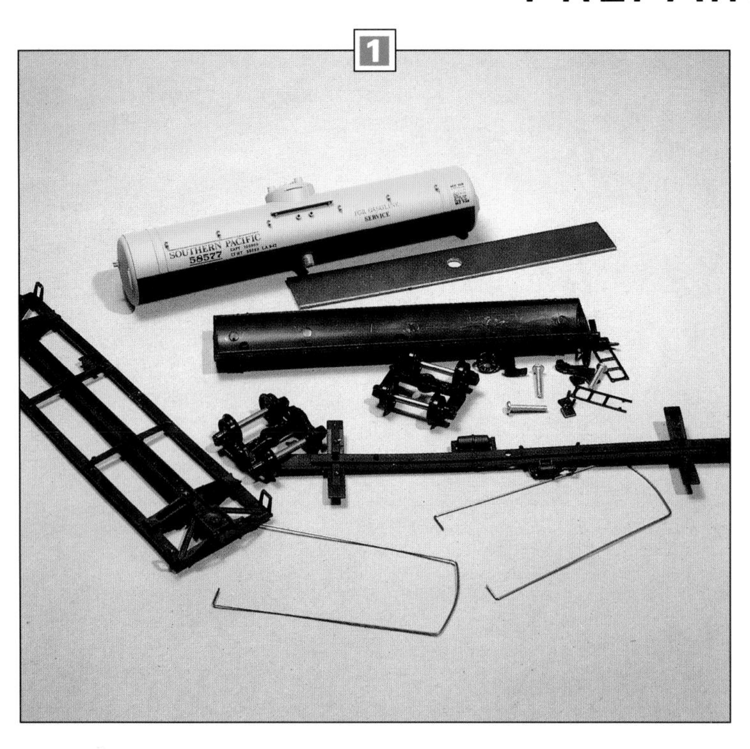


1 *These are the basic components of the kit: the pre-formed handrails, chassis pieces, trucks, and tank parts.*

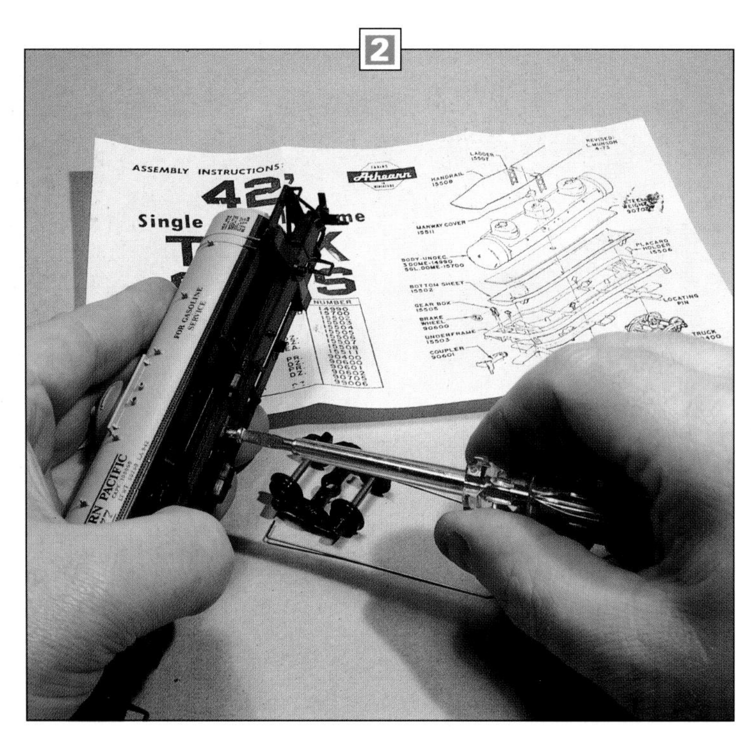


2 *The metal weight is placed inside the two halves of the tank, these are aligned, the chassis is held underneath, and all are then screwed together.*

3 *A screw secures each truck to the chassis, and the bottoms of the ladders are placed in the chassis slots on each side. The handrails clip to the sides of the tank, and the ends go through the holes in the tops of the ladders, securing them to the tank.*

4 *The end brake handle is simply pushed into the slot there to complete the tank car.*

# UNPAINTED KIT

**HELPFUL HINTS**

Use a glue dispenser which is fitted with a capillary tube – this allows easy access to joints.

When using superglue, always put a small amount out on a scrap of paper, then apply the glue with a toothpick.

Any plastic parts which are bent can be straightened if placed in warm water.

Always wash plastic parts before gluing as they will be covered in a release agent from the molds.

When gluing multiple parts together, allow at least eight hours' setting time between each operation.

**RIGHT**

**These American freight cars made from plastic kits have been lightly aged, as the real thing would not be pristine.**

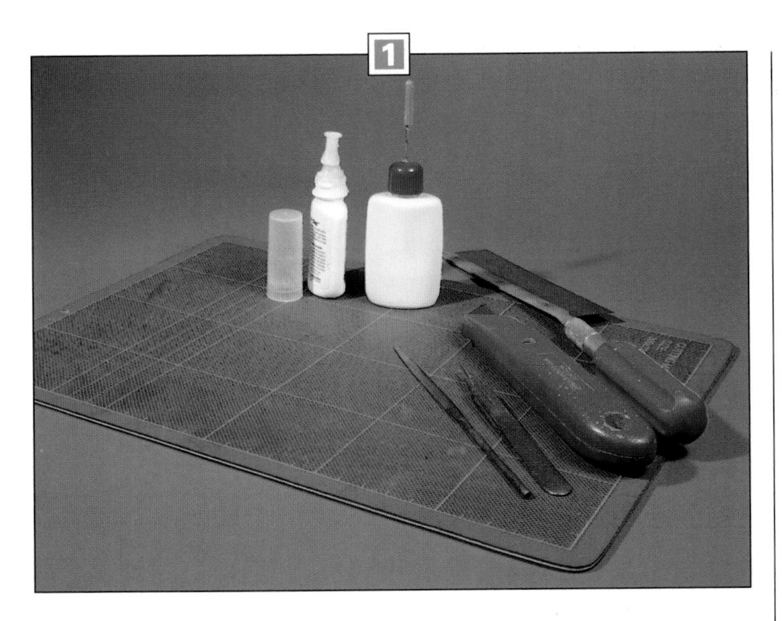

1 *The basic tools and materials needed to make this are straightforward: a cutting mat, which provides a good base to cut on, a small jeweler's saw, mat knife, small coarse file, tweezers, and glue. The main glue is specialist plastic glue, complete with a capillary dispenser, and the second is a superglue especially for plastic. Work in a well-ventilated room as the fumes from these glues can be powerful.*

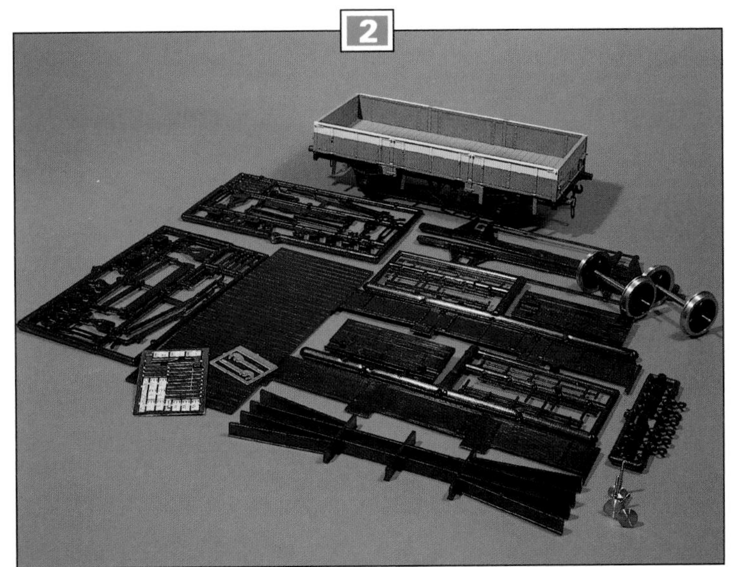

2 *The components of the kit include very detailed injection moldings, complete with rivet details, plus a small etched brass detailing fret. When completed, this kit produces the car shown at the top.*

3 *Using a jeweler's saw, the parts are carefully cut away from the sprue, resting it on the cutting mat as this is done.*

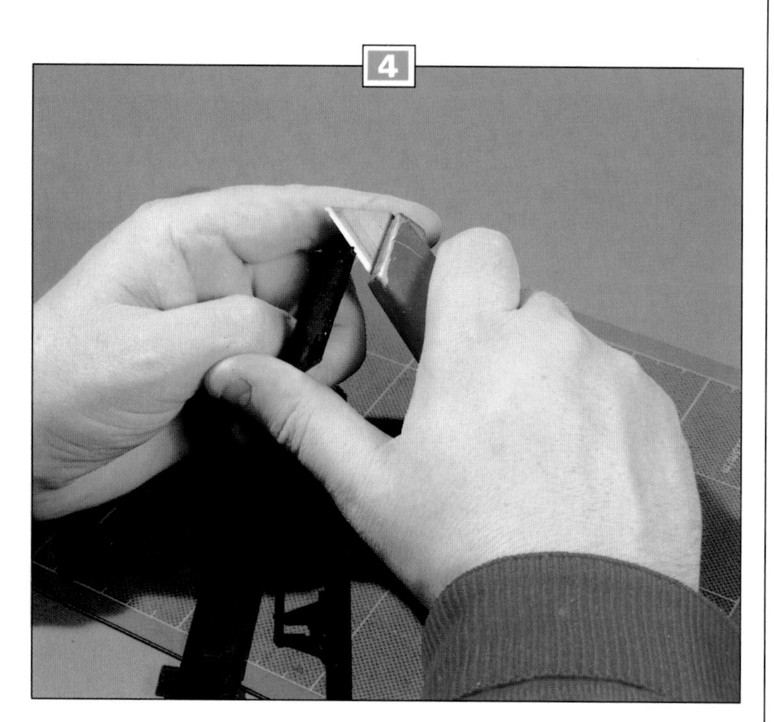


4 *When the parts have been separated, there are always a number of small bumps that need to be carefully removed using a mat knife.*

5 *One side and one end are held together against a carpenter's square to make sure that they are correctly aligned and then glued together down the inside of the joint with plastic glue. This is then repeated for the other three corners.*

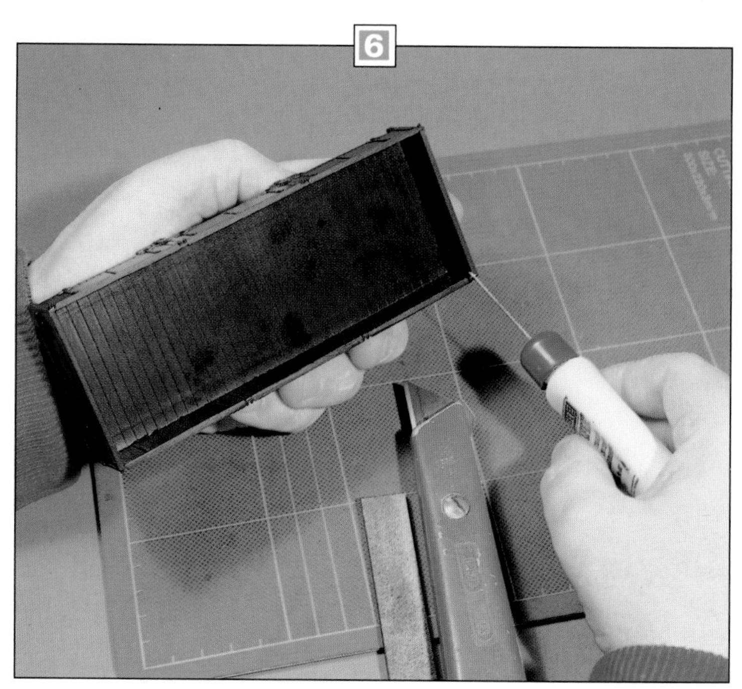


6 *When the glue is thoroughly dry, this frame is glued to the floor.*

7 *The side frames, axle guards, and axle boxes are cut out as before. The bearings are glued in, and the axle boxes are assembled and fitted into the side frames. The glue has to be applied very accurately as these parts need to move up and down. Also the brake handle and V-hanger are glued into place.*

8 *One of the side frames is glued to the main part of the wagon and left to set. The pairs of wheels are fitted into the glued side frame, and the other side frame is put into place on the other side, holding the wheels in position. Once it all seems to be square, the second side frame is glued.*

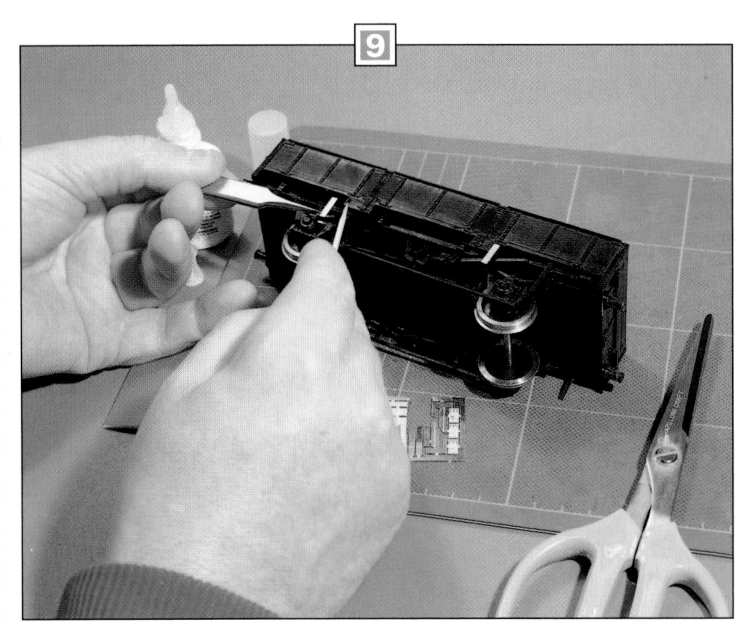

9 *The plastic superglue is used to secure the etched brass pieces to the plastic body. The technique for using the superglue is to press out a small quantity of the glue onto a scrap of paper and then to use a toothpick to dab a small amount of glue onto the area. The part is then pressed onto the glue and held there for several seconds while it sets.*

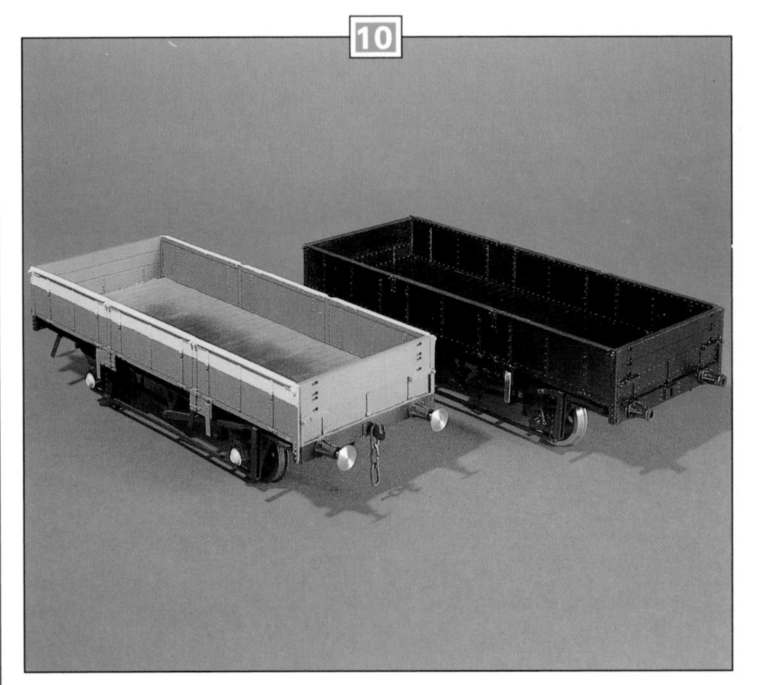

10 *On the right is the completed car, ready to be painted. On the left is the car once it has been painted, complete with sprung steel buffer heads.*

L N W
31688
31688
12 TONS
10 TONS
L N W R
10 TONS
L N W R

# CONSTRUCTING METAL KITS

**LEFT**

**Block trains are not a new concept. Here is a turn of the century freight yard full of cars built from metal kits.**

While it is possible to glue metal kits together, it is much better to solder them. Soldering has the great advantage that it can be undone easily. If one of the parts is incorrectly lined up or an angle is not quite square, then by applying a little heat, the parts can be gently moved to their correct positions or pulled apart, cleaned up, and soldered all over again. There are no such straightforward options with glues.

The step-by-step instructions in this chapter are for a brass kit, and they demonstrate the construction techniques involved in assembling metal kits. This kit has a number of white metal castings in it, so two methods of soldering metal are shown. The kit is basic in terms of the number of parts it has, but it requires pieces to be bent and formed, creating an interesting vehicle when it is finished.

**ABOVE**

**The fine selection of cars here are a mixture of etched brass kits (in the foreground) and all white metal ones (in the background).**

**RIGHT**

**Little homemade units like this may not look very beautiful, but are invaluable. The bottle of flux here is secured to a wide base so it cannot be knocked over, which is surprisingly easy to do when your other hand is holding the model steady.**

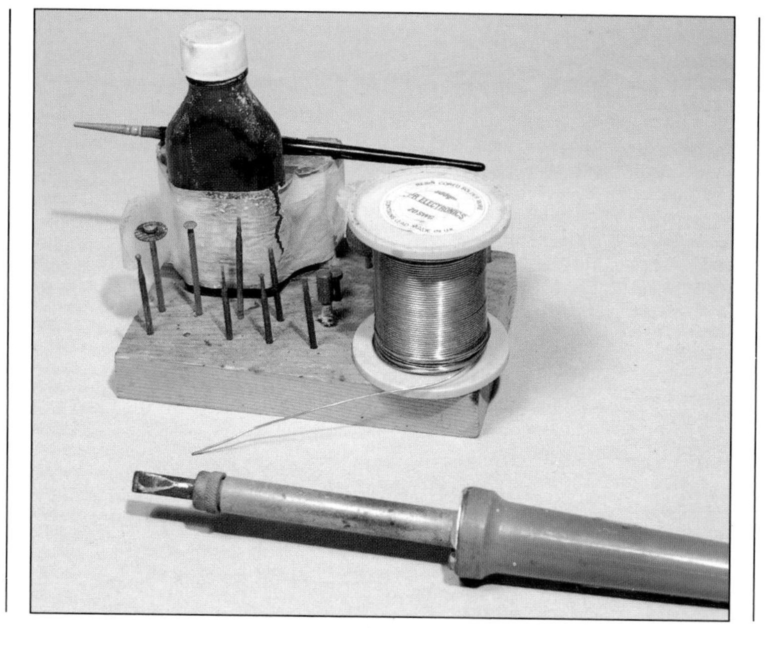

**HELPFUL HINTS**

When cutting out metal etches, be careful that you do not distort any of the components.

Metal surfaces that are to be soldered together should be cleaned, or the solder will not flow.

Always use a carpenter's square to check that construction is straight and upright.

During construction you can check that your structure is square by standing it on a piece of plate glass.

When soldering white metal to brass, always tin the brass with white metal solder first.

# METAL KIT

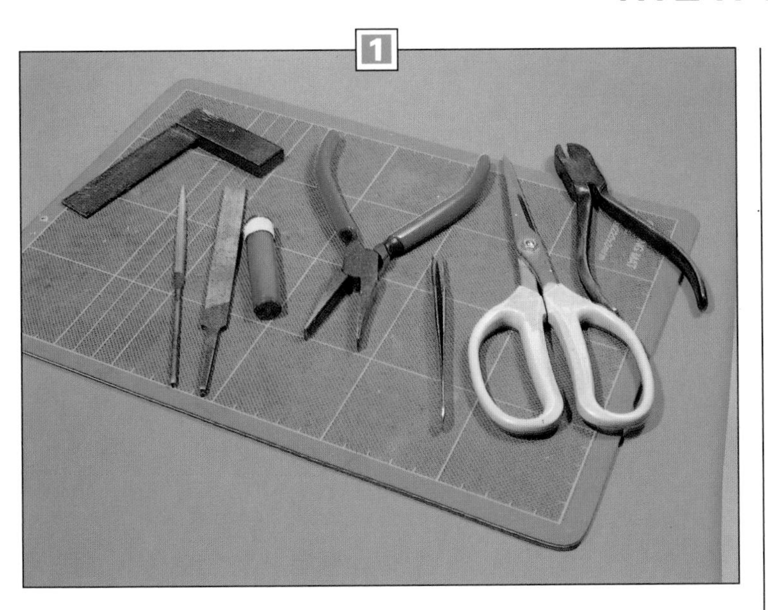

1 The tools needed to build metal kits do not need to be very specialized when you start out, although you will find that, as time goes on, you will acquire various tools that make the job easier and quicker. To begin with, however, all you need are: a cutting mat, scissors that will cut through metal, side snippers, tweezers, small- and medium-sized fine files, carpenter's square, glass fiber stick, and a good pair of wide-nosed pliers.

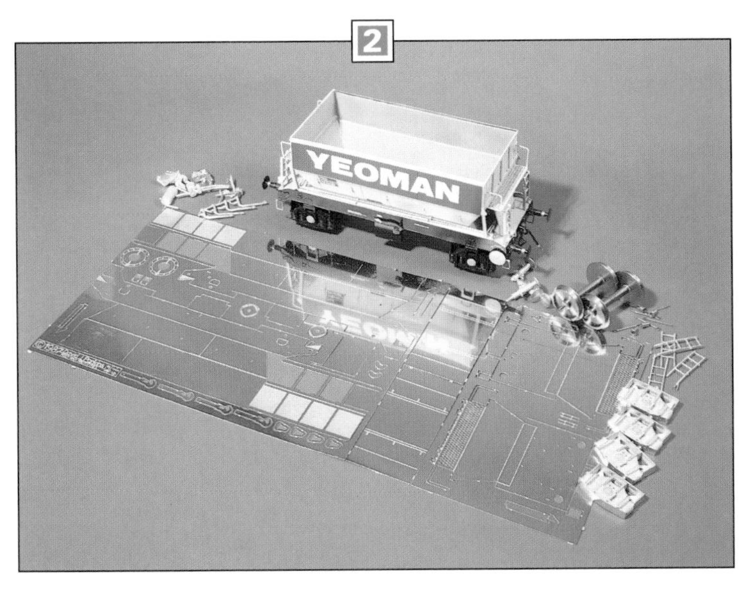


2 The components contained in the kit include the basic body of the wagon in etched brass; white metal castings for axle boxes, brake gear, and ladders; plus wheels, bearings, and couplings. When the kit is finished and painted, it produces the vehicle at the top.

3 Separating the parts from the sheet can be done in one of two ways, but whichever one is used, the parts being cut out must be supported and the cutting needs to be done extremely carefully. The large body parts can be removed using a sturdy pair of metal scissors.

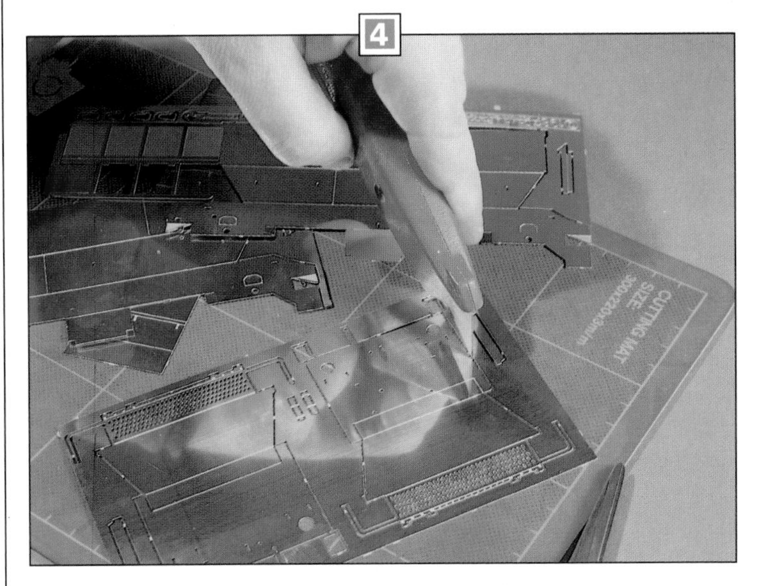


4 The finer, more inaccessible parts can be guillotined out using a mat knife. With the sheet on the cutting mat, the knife is placed with the point in front of the half-etched tab to be cut, then firmly brought down, cutting through the tab. This method causes the least amount of distortion of the metal. All the edges of the cutout brass pieces need to be cleaned up using a fine medium-sized file.

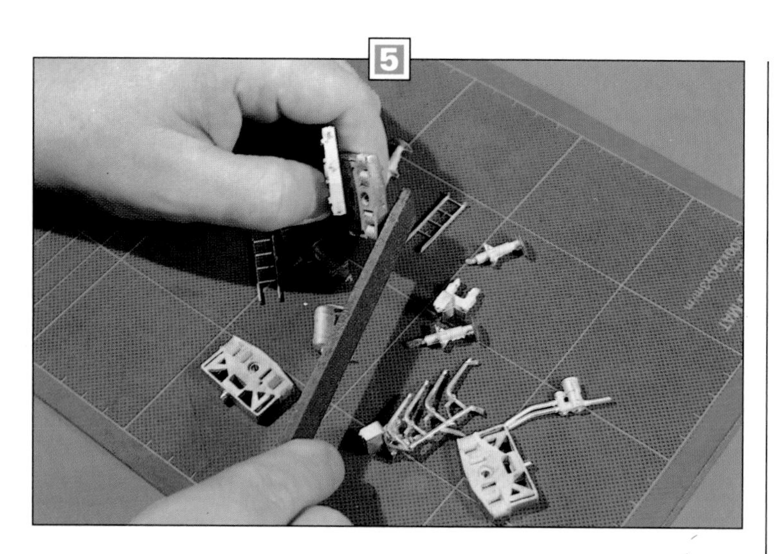

5 Next the white metal castings are cleaned up. The larger excess bumps can first be snipped off with the side cutters, then the area and other minor imperfections filed smooth with the coarser medium-sized file. When filing white metal, sprinkle some talcum powder on the file first, as this will help to prevent the metal from clogging the file. Repeat this application at reasonable intervals.

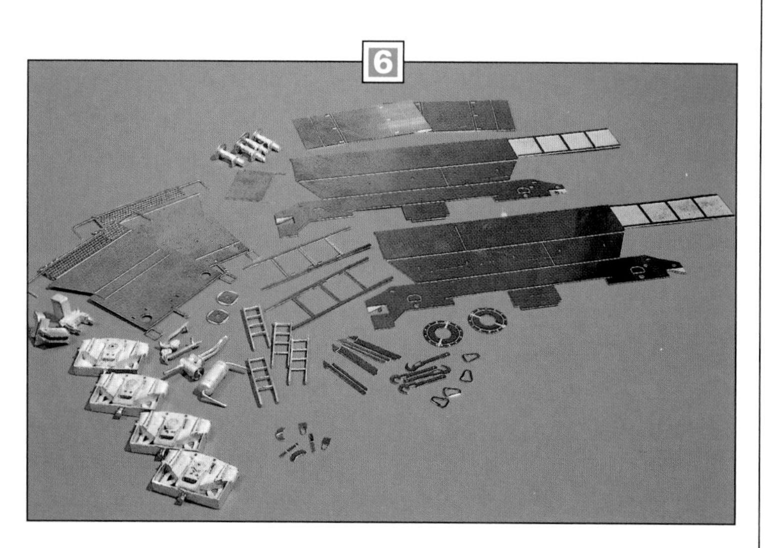

6 Here are all the components, ready to be fitted together.

7 At this stage it is useful to keep the instruction sheet and, if possible, some photographs of prototypes at hand, as the next stage is to start bending the pieces along the half-etched lines. For simple shapes, a good pair of wide, flat-nosed pliers are used to grip the part that needs to be folded.

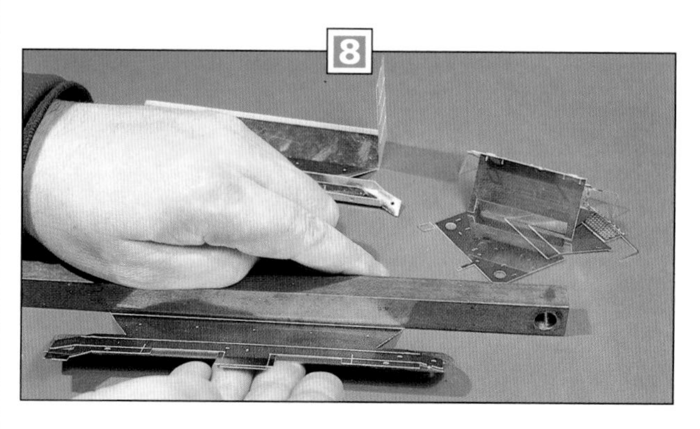

8 When the larger pieces need to be folded (such as the sides of the car), a length of square-section steel bar, long enough to be clamped down at both ends using small C-clamps, is very useful. A metal ruler is simply then placed under the other half of the piece to be bent and lifted. The metal on both sides of the foldline must be supported during the bending process.

9 Here are the pieces after they have been folded into the required shapes.

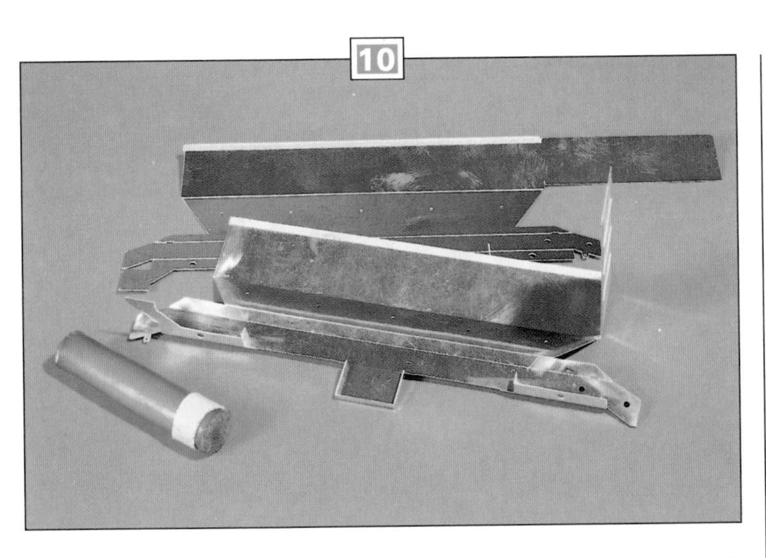

10 *Successful soldering is dependent on good clean edges. Thus, at this stage, a glass fiber stick is rubbed up and down the edges that will be soldered together to prepare them.*

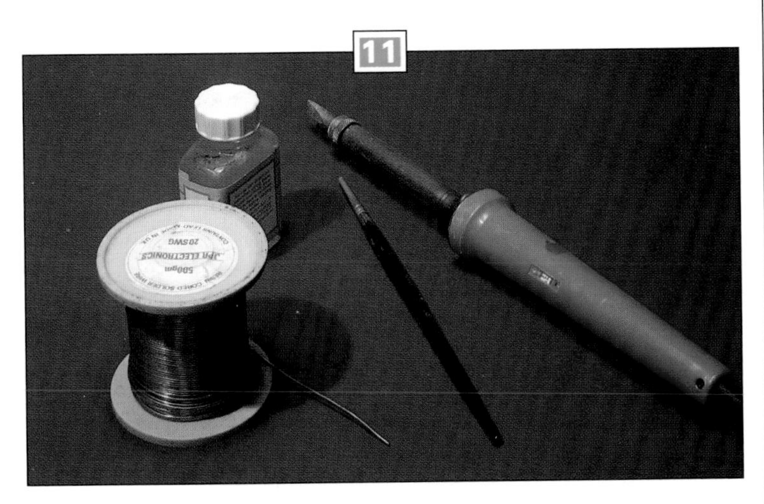

11 *Soldering irons are simple tools, and it is a matter of personal preference as to which one and what wattage you choose. A 100-watt iron will supply plenty of heat that can be applied to the job, melt the solder and run it down the joint, and remove it all in a short space of time. There are modelers, though, who prefer to use smaller irons and a lower temperature solder, so it is up to you. Also required is a good liquid flux, which transfers the heat, and a small paintbrush to apply it to the area to be soldered. It has to be used with care as it attacks metal surfaces.*

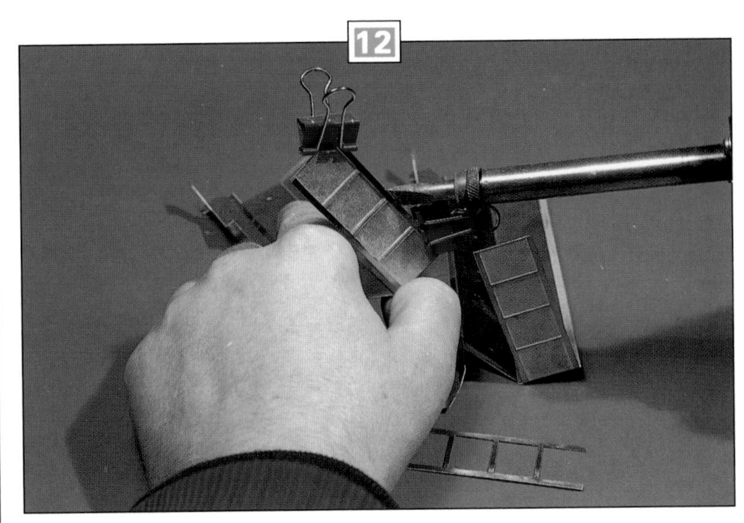

12 *The first job is to solder the fine skeleton overlay to the end of one side. The two items are clamped in place with spring clips, and the alignment is checked several times (to cut down on mistakes and the frustration of getting it wrong). The flux is carefully painted along the edges, then a small amount of solder is melted onto the tip of the soldering iron and applied to the joint. The clips are removed when the metal parts have cooled down, then the joint is cleaned up using a file.*

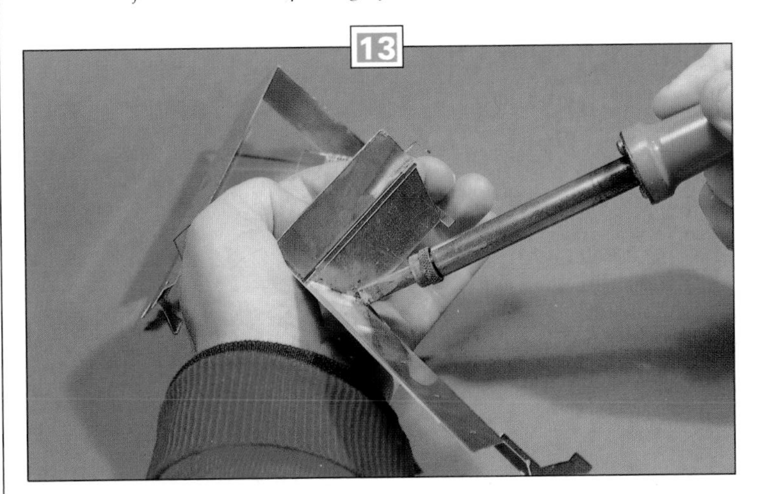

13 *When one of the ends is being soldered to a side, it has to be held firmly in position, and spots of solder are applied at the top and bottom of the joint to hold it in place. Then, when it has been checked and is found to be square, the full length of the joint is soldered by running the solder from one end to the center, letting it cool, then repeating this from the other end to the center and letting it cool.*

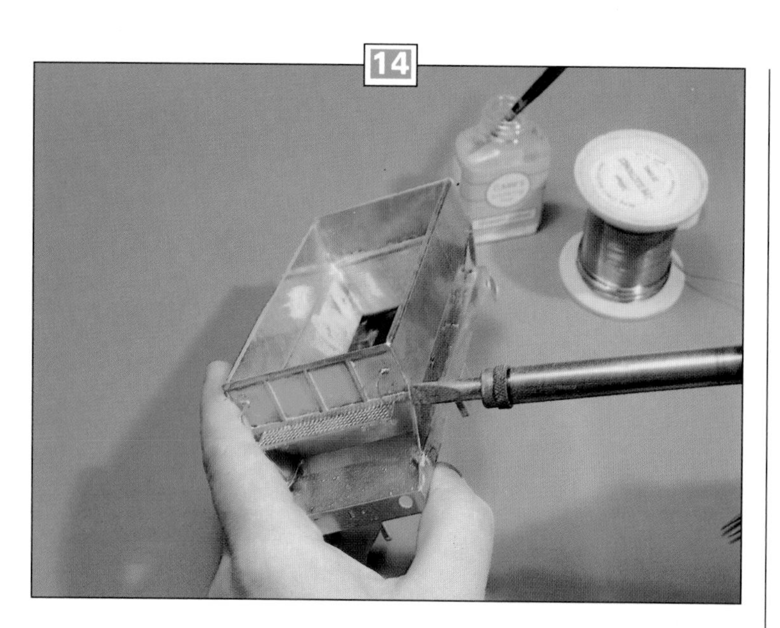

14 The pairs of ends and sides are joined together, checking them first to make sure they echo each other perfectly. For the joint illustrated, a little flux is dribbled down inside the car, and the soldering iron, loaded with melted solder, is run along the outside of the joint. The flux will draw the solder through the joint, forming a neat filling of the joint. Any excess solder on the outside can be cleaned off easily using a file.

15 Smaller brass components are soldered into place by first painting a little flux on the area that is to be attached, positioning the part on this area, then touching any flux seeping around the part with the soldering iron so that the solder is drawn under the part, securing it to the body.

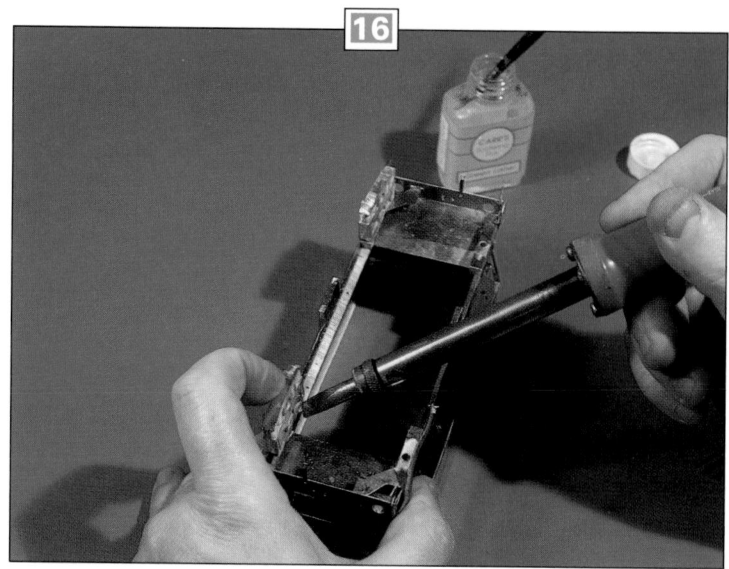

16 For the white metal castings, a lower temperature soldering iron and solder is used, but the techniques for joining pieces are the same as before. Flux is painted onto the parts to be joined; then the loaded soldering iron is used, touching the brass side of the joint and the solder then flows between the two metals. The soldering iron is then removed, and the parts are left to cool before they are moved. This takes a lot longer than for joining brass to brass.

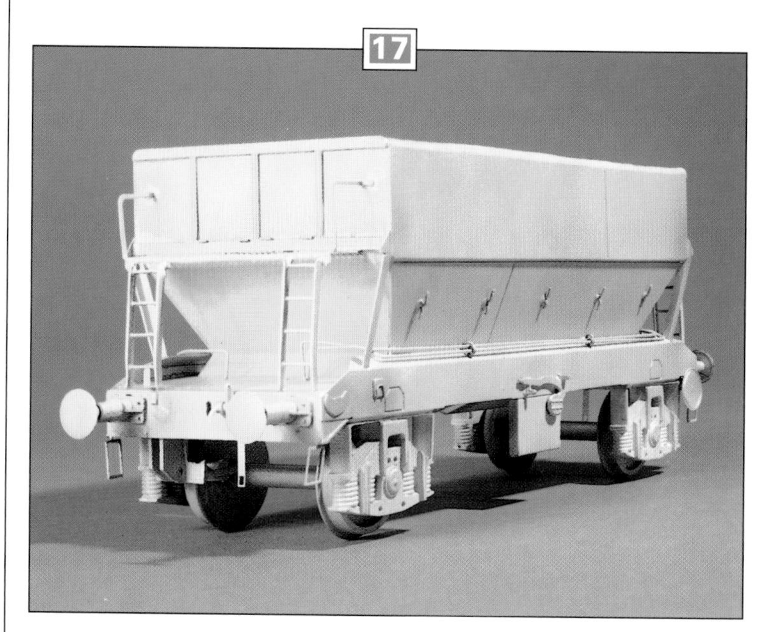

17 Here is the completed car, with all the white metal castings in position, ready to be painted.

**ABOVE**

This is the ultimate in railcar construction. This masterpiece 0-gauge model was built by expert modeler Jim Whittaker. Every single piece of it has been handmade, and the accuracy is astounding – even down to the rivets!

**LEFT**

This brass boxcar is incredibly detailed, and all of these tiny pieces have been soldered on. Such fine detail is only possible when such a model is made from brass. It is also very strong.

neb+w
BERKSHIRE LINES
Milwaukee, Racine & Troy
ARTZ

# PAINTING AND WEATHERING

**LEFT**
**It is not only rolling stock that needs to be weathered. Buildings also need this treatment so that they fit into the overall scene.**

For some reason many modelers are very wary of painting. Just as soldering is really quite straightforward when approached with due care, painting, too, is an extremely rewarding aspect of the hobby. If the worst comes to the worst, the model can always be stripped down, and you can start all over again.

While many people are adept at brushing on paint, few can match the uniform finish produced by an airbrush. Although they are expensive items of equipment, they do last and so are a good investment when you consider that, with practice, the finish you can achieve is unequalled.

Airbrushes with a double-action feature allow the user to control the paint and air flow mixture completely ~ you push down for air and pull back for paint. Compressors can be used to supply a constant source of air, but air cans can be used instead until you can afford this piece of equipment.

When spraying, the room must be well-ventilated, and a small mask should be worn to avoid inhaling too much paint vapor. If a lot of painting is being done regularly, building a small spray booth with an extractor fan is a wise idea.

Before spraying, the model must be scrupulously cleaned; otherwise, finger marks or other smudges will show as slightly different color, spoiling the finish. It is well worth taking time at this stage for the difference it makes to the completed model.

# PAINTING A KIT

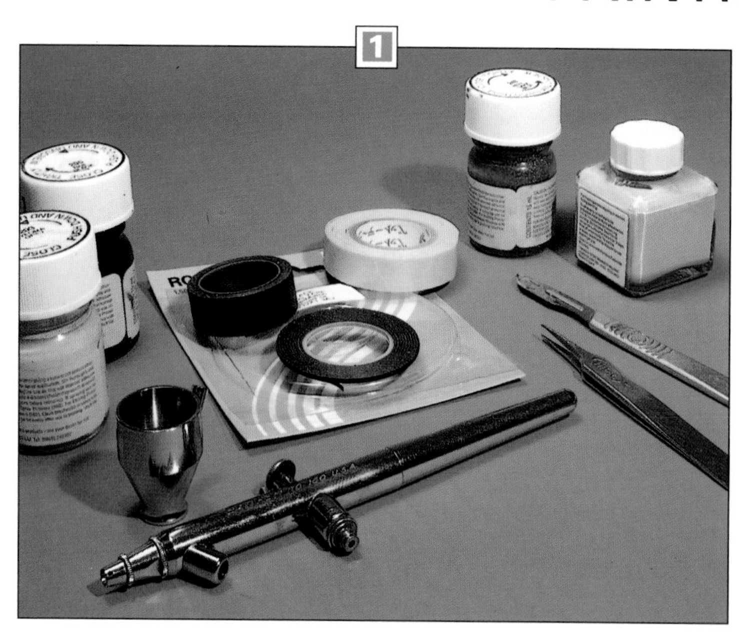

1 *These are the basic materials that were used to paint the PGA car shown in Chapter 8: an airbrush, complete with side cup, paints, and thinners; several widths of masking and lining tape; and masking fluid, tweezers, and mat knife.*

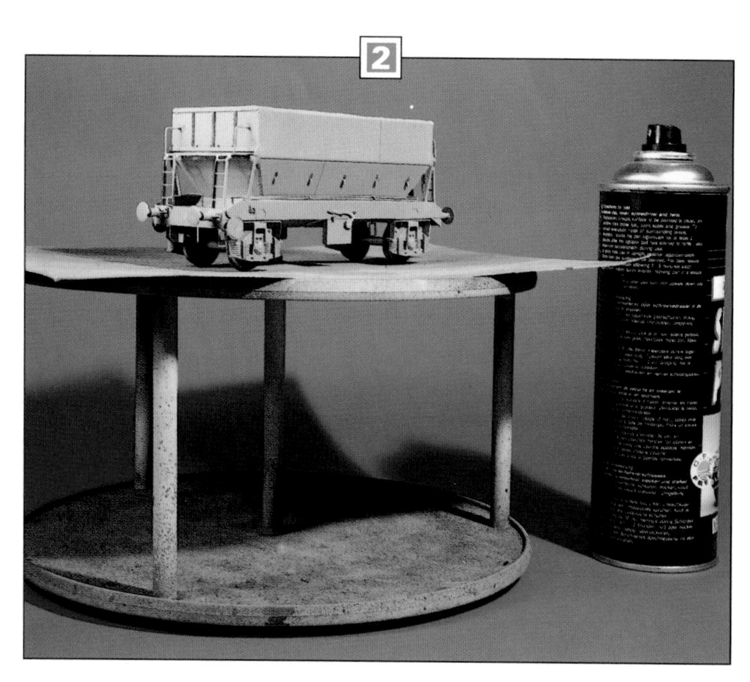

2 *One useful piece of equipment is this cake stand-type table, sometimes called a storage stand. It rotates, enabling the model to be sprayed from all sides without having to handle it.*

3 *Once the model has been thoroughly cleaned, given a good wash and rinse in soapy water, and then left to dry thoroughly, the primer is applied. Aerosol paints used for priming car bodywork can be used for this purpose. The can must be shaken well before the paint is applied. Spray a sample first to make sure that it has been mixed enough.*

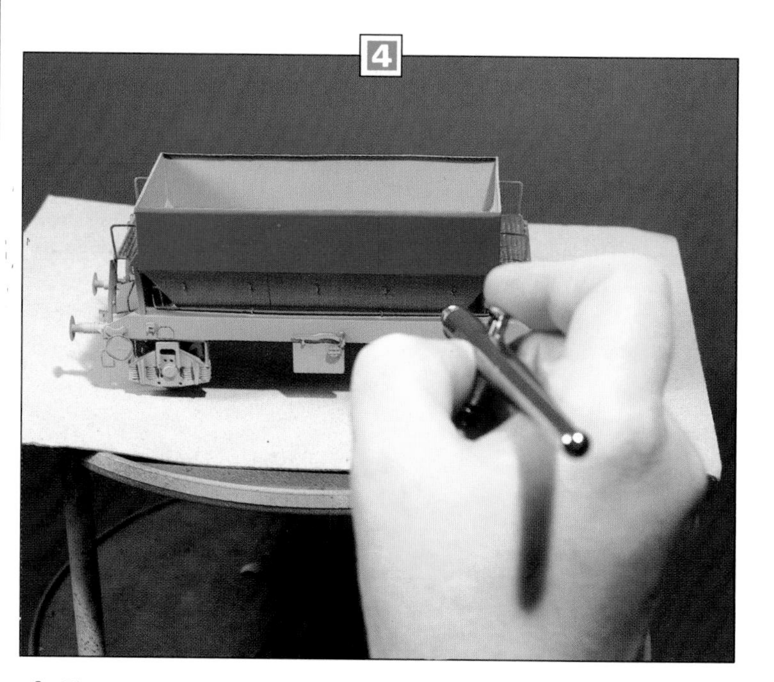

4 *First a coat of blue paint is applied to the top half of the car. This area will eventually carry the owner's logo. The paint is mixed with an equal quantity of thinners (the paint should be the consistency of milk). Then even coats are sprayed across the model, starting and stopping the spray of paint outside of the edges of the model to avoid splattering.*

5 *Once the paint has dried (at least eight hours should be allowed between each application), this first color can be masked. This system is known as* reverse masking. *Starting at the end of one of the longest sides, using 3/16-in (5-mm) wide lining tape, the end is held down on the model, stretched along the length of the side, then gently pressed down, making sure it is perfectly straight (a metal ruler is used to check this). The lining tape is applied along the other long side in the same way, ensuring as this is done that the lines are parallel. The end strips are then stuck down in the same way. No little bits of tape should overhang the shape at the corners – these must be made perfectly square with a mat knife or sharp scissors.*

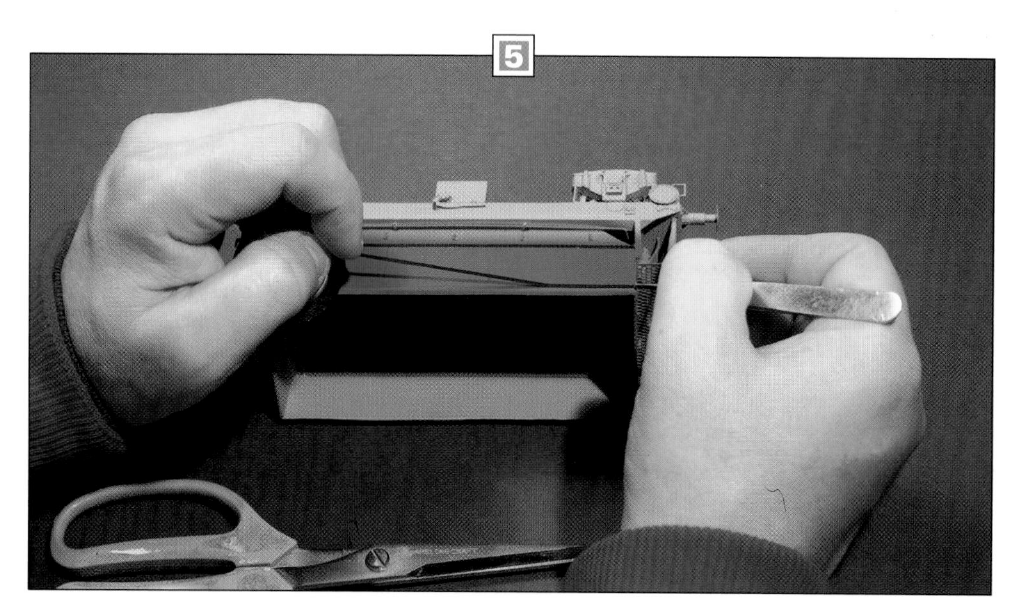

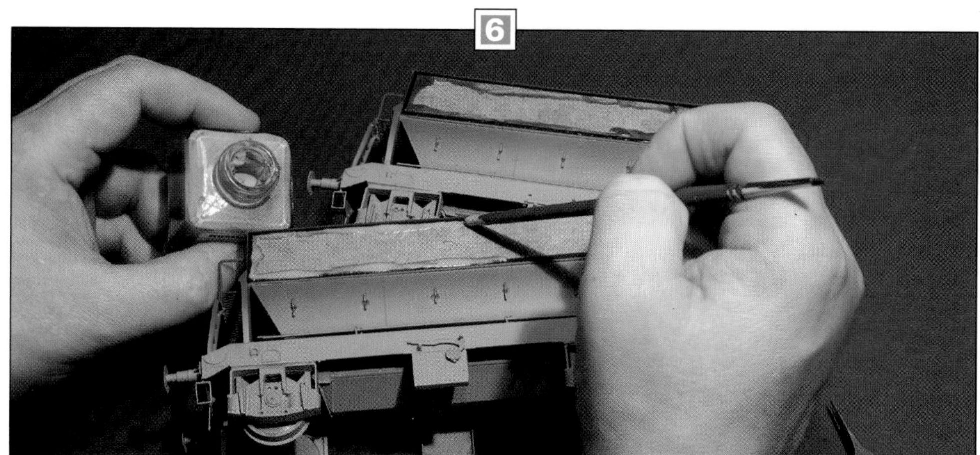

6 *The central area is now masked off using ordinary wide masking tape. It does not have to meet the lining tape, in fact, leaving a gap is fine. To make a 100 percent spray-tight joint between the lining and masking tapes, masking fluid is painted over the gap between the two tapes, sealing both edges. This is left to dry (it changes color as it dries, and a thin film takes a matter of minutes to dry).*

7 *The next color to be applied is black for the chassis. The model has to be held in the hand in order to spray underneath (covering your hand with a plastic bag is wise). The model is left for eight hours while the paint dries.*

**HELPFUL HINTS**

Thoroughly clean any model before painting by washing it in soapy water and then rinsing in warm water.

Use a suitable rotating stand to spray models on, for example, a cake icing stand.

If you are spraying, make sure the room is well-ventilated, and remember to wear a mask.

Allow at least eight hours between each color application so the paint can harden properly.

Always varnish your model after applying transfers to seal them and so stop curling.

8 *Using the same technique as before, the black area is masked off. When deciding which area to mask, it is best to opt for the easiest areas – spraying a light color over a dark one is easy wi:h an airbrush.*

9 *Using the spraying table, the model is placed in the center of it and sprayed light gray. Spraying several thin coats allows the color to be built up to cover the blue without the danger of smothering any of the fine detail on the car, which is more likely to happen if a brush was used.*

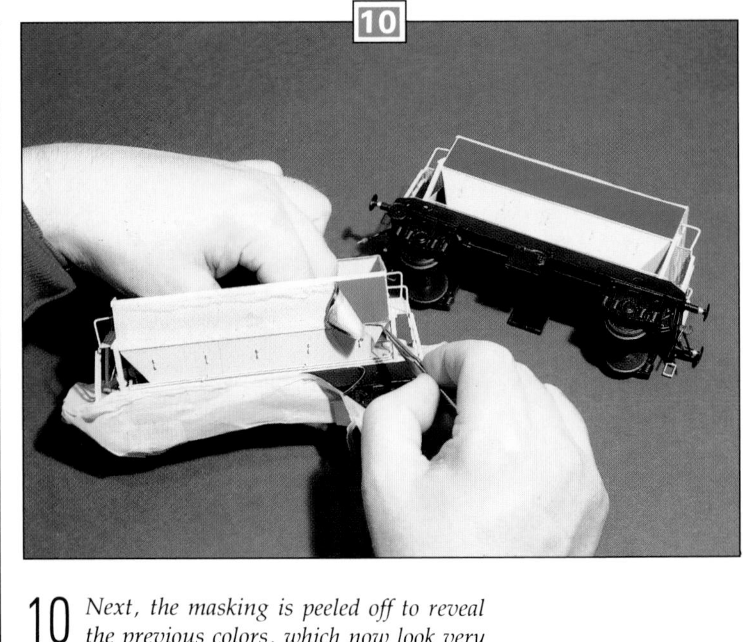


10 *Next, the masking is peeled off to reveal the previous colors, which now look very precise, with strong, clean edges. Because the last application of paint is usually to the largest area, it is a good idea to remove the masking when the paint is still a little soft.*

11 *Some of the finer details are picked out with a fine paintbrush. Here, the white steps and brake wheel are being painted. The circular axle box bosses are picked out in yellow later.*

# APPLYING TRANSFERS AND WEATHERING

## APPLYING TRANSFERS

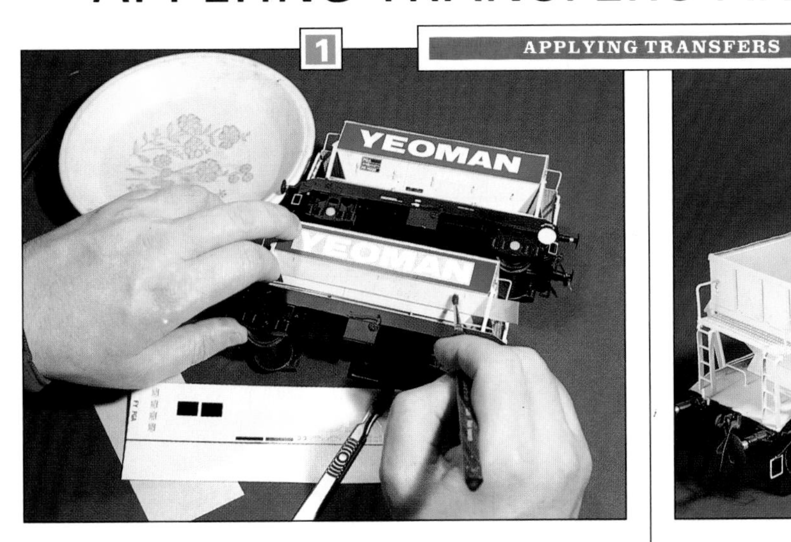


1 *Applying transfers is not as tricky as people think if a few guidelines are followed. Here, press and fix-style transfers of the private owner's name are being applied. First, a piece of masking tape is marked with the length of the name, and the center point is marked. This is centered on the side of the car to act as a guide for positioning the transfer, which then only has to be centered vertically. The transfer is then positioned and pressed firmly. The backing is brushed with water, so it becomes soft and is easily lifted off.*

2 *When their interiors have been lightly sprayed in an aluminum or steel color, and the whole of each car has been varnished to protect the transfers, the finished vehicles look convincing.*

## WEATHERING

1 *Regarding weathering, how much should be applied is a matter of personal choice. Some modelers like to apply it heavily, while others like just a fine dusting. If the aim is to make the model just like the real thing, then the roofs and chassis need quite heavy applications of "dirt." There are two ways of applying weathering: by painting it on and by using weathering powders. They can be used together, too. The roof and chassis of this train have already been lightly airbrushed with a dusty color that has been very well thinned down, and now highlights are being picked out using dusting powders.*

2 *Weathering of these boxcars has been achieved by giving them a very light spray of thinned-down weathering paint. The right effect cannot always be achieved in one pass. Instead, the weathered areas may need to be built up in several coats.*

PEN-THAVEN BRIDGE
GREAT WESTERN
SOUTHERN
337
PARKINSON
MERCHANTS
TUDHOPE
GRAVESEND
41
CORRALL & Co Ltd
BRIGHTON
321

# BUILDING A LOCOMOTIVE

**LEFT**

**The Great Western "Mogul" arrives, and the ex-LSWR 4-4-0 departs with the Southern Region train. These locomotives have been expertly built and finished, and are a pleasure to behold.**

The techniques for constructing the metal car described in the previous chapter are essentially the same as those used for building a locomotive. This 4 mm HO/00 scale Claughton kit has more white metal castings for the bodywork than the wagon, but the best way of building it is to solder the pieces together. If gluing is preferred, however, any of the two-part epoxy resin glues would be ideal for this type of kit. They are used by mixing equal amounts of two parts, which can be squeezed out onto a scrap of cardboard and mixed thoroughly. When applying the glue, put a very thin film onto both of the surfaces to be joined, then carefully bring the parts together and remove any excess, making sure that the parts are square. Put to one side and allow 24 hours to dry before carrying out any more construction on these parts. This lengthy drying time means that it is best to try to build everything in sub-units.

# BUILDING A LOCOMOTIVE

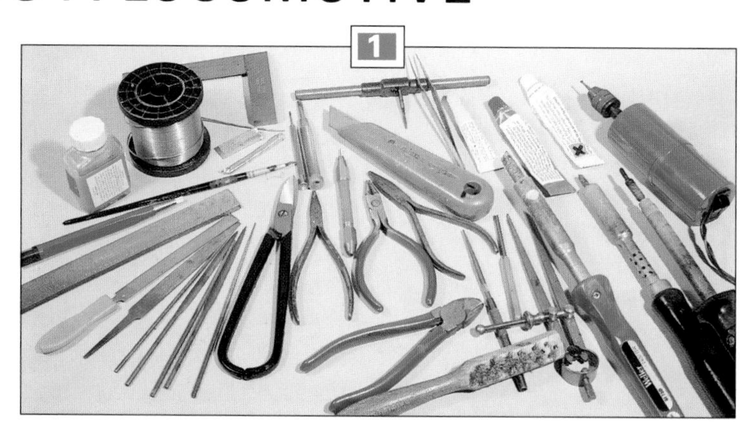


1 *A wider selection of tools is used in this project than in the metal kit construction. While essentially more of certain items are featured, such as files, the main additions are an electric drill for drilling or enlarging holes in the etches. Along with the various pliers are tin snips – ideal for cutting the metal from frets. Also featured is two-part epoxy resin glue used for adding fittings.*

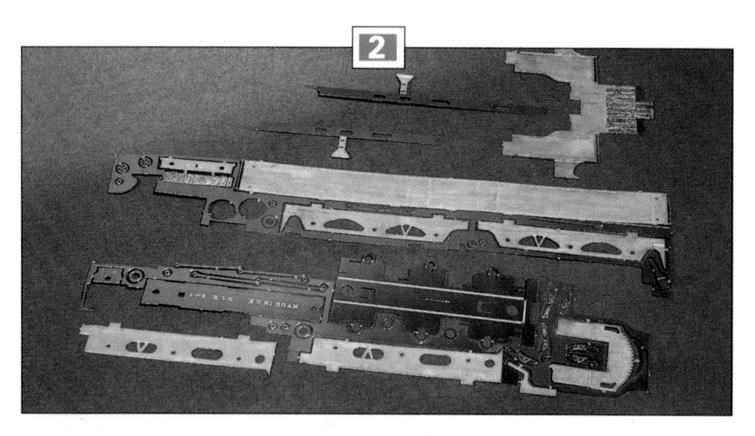


2 *The principal etched brass parts are for the tender chassis, body, main frames, and foot-plate valances. This type of kit makes the most of the positive aspects of each type of metal: for detail and flatness, etched brass is best.*

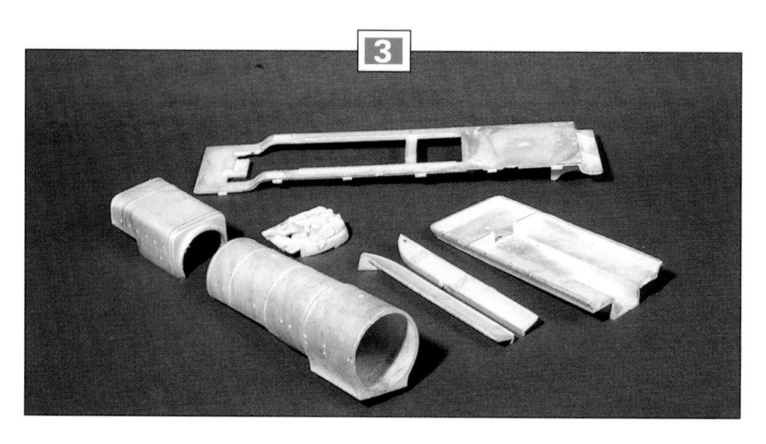


3 *Here are the major white metal castings for the tender top, engine footplate, firebox and boiler/smokebox assembly. These are carefully filed to make them smooth* *(see page 70)**. Then all the pieces are checked to make sure that a good fit exists between the parts to be glued or soldered together.*

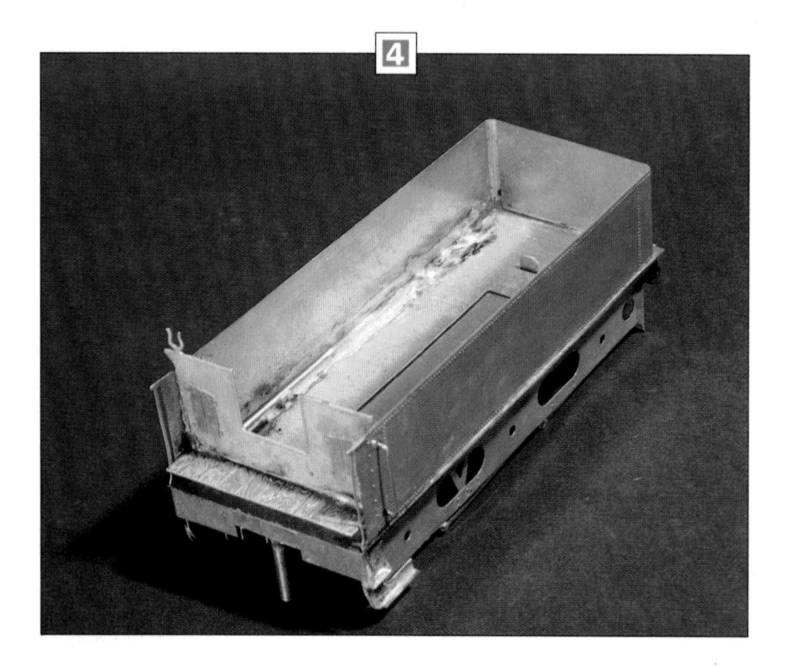


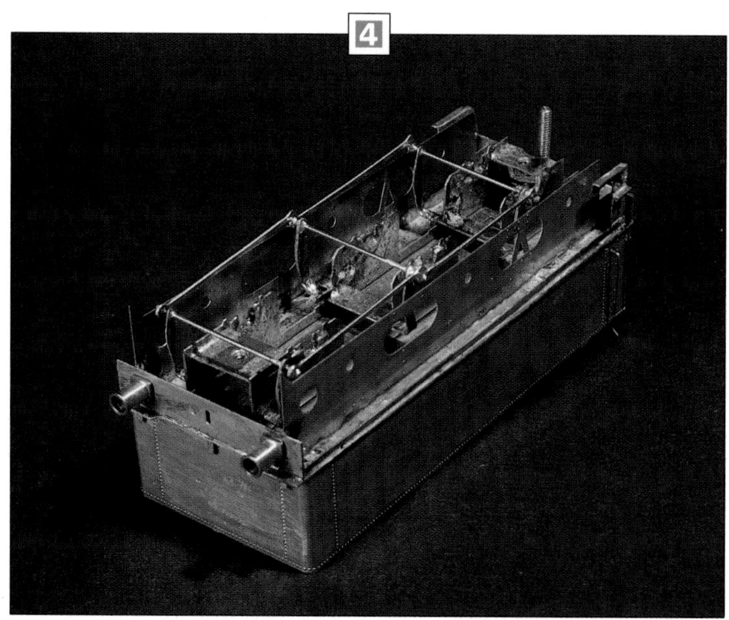


4 *Here are views of the top and underside of coal car and engine chassis during assembly.*

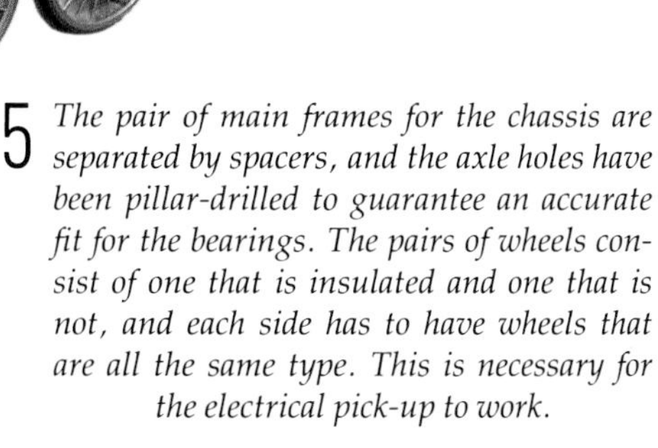

5 *The pair of main frames for the chassis are separated by spacers, and the axle holes have been pillar-drilled to guarantee an accurate fit for the bearings. The pairs of wheels consist of one that is insulated and one that is not, and each side has to have wheels that are all the same type. This is necessary for the electrical pick-up to work.*

**HELPFUL HINTS**

Whether gluing or soldering, parts to be joined together should always be thoroughly cleaned first.

Where possible, always build in sub-assemblies.

Paint the chassis – usually black – before (not after) the wheels are fitted.

Check that construction is square, but more important, check that the smokestack, dome, and safety valve are in line and lean backward or forward.

Allow enough sideplay on the wheelsets so the chassis can negotiate the minimum radius on the layout.

6 *The basic body parts, both etched brass and white metal castings, have been soldered together. Though the instructions split the construction of the engine and coal car, it is, in fact, a good idea to build the two parts at the same time to make sure that they fit squarely together.*

7 *The final details to be added to the engine are the dome, smokestack and safety valves, plus the handrails and the smaller castings. Unless it is possible to get to the back of these castings with a soldering iron, it is best to just glue them into place.*

8 *The finished model needs to be thoroughly cleaned and dried prior to painting to result in a first-class finish.*

9 *The completed locomotive, painted in fully lined LMS crimson lake livery, shows just how handsome these elegant locomotives were.*

**RIGHT**

**The paintwork on any locomotive will make or break an excellently built model, so it is worth taking care at that stage to avoid spoiling the efforts made during the construction process.**

LEFT

Still in its unfinished brass state, this Pennsylvania electric switch engine has been constructed flawlessly.

HOT
BEL-AIR
HOTEL
NEW HAVEN
3342
S.F.R.D.

11

# CONSTRUCTING BUILDINGS

**LEFT**
**This masterpiece in HO scale cleverly combines both brick and concrete buildings.**

Model railroad buildings generally fall into three main categories: buildings "owned" by the railroad, private buildings on, or adjacent to, railroad property, and connected with the railroad's business, and the rest. Railroad property will, of course, feature in most layouts, but it is advisable to round out the picture a little and include other types of buildings. Those falling into the third category are, essentially, there to justify the existence of the railroad. It is easy to think, though, after seeing layouts beautifully adorned with realistic-looking buildings, that unless there is a town close by, the model is lacking something.

There are plenty of kits readily available for the modeler. Many railroad building kits are made from printed cards. Some of these, designed for quick assembly, are, perhaps, a little lacking in subtlety and need some very careful extra work if they are to look their best.

Some companies are now producing plastic kits as well as completed buildings. They can be a little too toy-like for the real enthusiast, but they are well proportioned and can be developed and enhanced to fill a gap on the layout.

# CARDBOARD BUILDING KIT

1 *A station building kit is an ideal first-time project with which to feel your way into building construction. These are made from heavy cardboard and come flat packed. Once the main parts of the building have been folded up, it is imperative to get the walls and ends square and perpendicular. The use of a metal square and steel ruler will help accomplish this.*

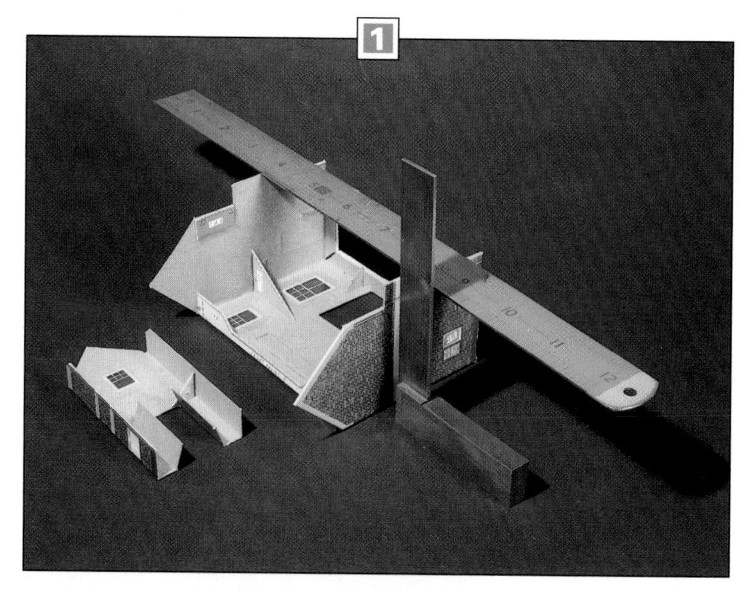

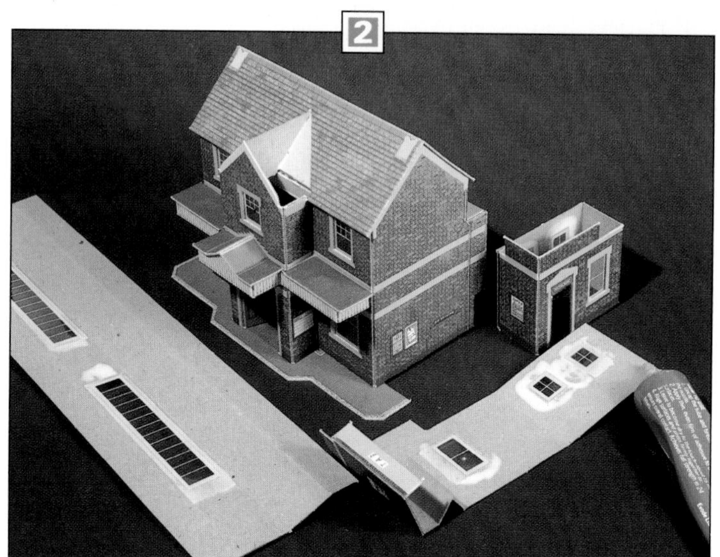

2 *Here the windows, once they have been carefully cut out, are glued to the correct openings while the walls are flat. Once the glue is dry, the buildings can be formed.*

3 *This is a simple way of producing convincing buildings and as can be seen from the result, they look good when completed.*

**LEFT**

This period freight storage building is built to scale and really captures the character of its time. Built entirely from plastic card, the inside is as detailed as the exterior.

**BELOW**

This Austrian scene in HO scale uses one of the many well-detailed European plastic building kits available.

With little more than just cosmetic changes, most plastic kits can be successfully adapted in ways their designers probably never thought of. Lines of industrial structures that have a strong common bond in terms of a standard pattern of wall and substantially similar doors and windows are ideally suited for mixing and matching as required. Some very impressive large industrial buildings have been created by combining several kits.

The absence of a myriad of instantly suitable kits is no great tragedy, for model railroads call for variety and individuality, so however big the choice might be, there would still be something missing from it as far as *your* layout was concerned. Around most railroad stations, there is a welter of different kinds of buildings – sometimes in the final stages of decay, sometimes in prime condition. As a result, the modeler's imaginative rendering of such individuality is not limited in any way. Further, if the architecture of another country appeals to you, there is no reason at all for not making a model of a stretch of railroad in that country and using appropriate models for it. Even with the increased range of options this will open up, there will no doubt be particular buildings that you will want to make yourself.

The traditional materials for making model buildings are cardboard and plywood, but more recently plastic card has become very popular. This is very probably because it is available in sheets with all kinds of embossed textures, including bricks, shingles, street surfaces, paving stones, walling, planking . . . the list goes on. This saves modelers a great deal of time and is usually more realistic than textures produced by other means. Also, it is an easy

**BELOW**

**Patience and tremendous woodcraft skills are needed to undertake the construction of a model like this.**

**ABOVE**

**This model of a traditional terrace of shops in the north of England is built from cardboard covered in paper that has a brick pattern printed on it. The buildings have then been carefully painted.**

**HELPFUL HINTS**

When joining walls at right angles, add triangular strengtheners inside.

From time to time throughout construction, check that the components of your buildings are square.

After cardboard buildings have been folded up, use a pen of the correct color to hide the white fold line.

Where possible, extend the building walls below ground level so they have to be planted in position – this gets rid of the problem of a visible gap between the bottom of the building and the ground.

Putting a small light in one of the rooms will bring any building to life.

medium to cut and glue. However, extreme care must be exercised when using the specialist glues required, as the vapor from them is quite powerful, so working in a well-ventilated room and for short periods of time is imperative.

An example of just what can be achieved is Shirley Rowe's major piece of work – a layout based in Spain. She visited this area when she went there for a vacation and was so inspired by what she saw that she made this model. She told me how she went about designing and building it.

Along the coastal line on which Sant Pol station is situated is a long string of resorts, but no one particular station was crying out to be made into a diorama. However, each had attractive features, and there were other towns, away from the rail line, that possessed a wealth of buildings worthy of

**ABOVE**

**This drawing of the Catalunya layout gives a good idea of just how much building was involved. The numbered arrows show the positions from which the photographs below and on page 93 were taken.**

modeling. A composite scene was consequently decided on for the final diorama, the features of which were drawn from five locations in the area.

Photographs of more buildings than could ever be fitted into a diorama were taken with the intention of having a vast selection of "possibles" to draw from when the time for planning it all came.

At Sant Pol, there is a tunnel at the end of the platform, but the buildings on the hill above were not very pleasant to look at. At Tossa, however, there was similar rocky headland jutting out from the beach with impressive castle walls and turrets built on the rocks, but no railroad nearby. Both locations were photographed in the hope that the two might be combined.

At home, all the photographs were laid out, and the best buildings were chosen. Then their positions were decided by putting them on the floor in the approximate places that they would occupy in the diorama.

To help the planning process, a mini-diorama was made from cardboard, including the cabinet – a base with sides and back added, but with the front left open. The landscape and buildings were modeled in styrofoam to a scale of 1:750. This established the beach, tracks, station, headland, tunnel, and castle walls, together with favorite buildings, as being the essential elements. Although they were only crudely modeled pieces of styrofoam, it was easy

**ABOVE**

**View of the railroad line from the seashore. Note the lack of fencing around the track, a typical feature of Spanish railroads.**

**LEFT**

**A view from above the layout, looking directly up the line toward the station.**

ABOVE

A view which shows the variety of rooftops on the buildings directly behind the station.

ABOVE

Steps running up to houses and apartments near the ruin.

LEFT

Boats moored in the bay below the ruin.

LEFT

Small houses positioned near the shore next to the station.

to see exactly which of the "runner-up" buildings would fit around the favorites to complete the scene.

The stretch of coast from Barcelona to Tossa de Mar includes Pineda, Sant Pol, Malgrat, and three other resorts all bearing the suffix "de Mar," so it was decided that this imaginary composite town's name would also be a "de Mar." There were to be castle walls on the headland, and she had visited the inland village of Castellet, so the station is Castellet de Mar. Why, then, the name of *Catalunya* for the whole layout? Well, she had had an exciting and interesting vacation in Spain, exploring what in English is known as the "Catalonia" region, but she noticed that local maps spelled it "Catalunya," which she liked much more, hence the name.

The station was tackled first, then the buildings nearest to it. She made these from plastic card, but the later structures were her first experiments in cardboard construction. There were so many buildings to make that it took about two and a half years to complete them all.

Then, at last, it was time to make a base for the diorama. It needed to be sturdy as it had to be in one piece, measuring 3½ × 8 ft (2.4 × 1.06 m). There had to be a flat surface at the front for the sea, beach, track, and road area; but the rear half is simply blocks of styrofoam glued to the wooden frame. She had never laid track before, but the hobby board she used for the surface takes track pins easily and with such a simple track plan, it was not difficult to do.

The large styrofoam blocks were stuck down to produce the shape of the castle headland, and holes were cut to hold the bases of the castle towers and the walls. These had been constructed from featherboard (otherwise known as foamboard or polyboard). This consists of two layers of cardboard sandwiching an ⅛-, 5⁄32- or 3⁄16-in (3-, 4- or 5-mm) core of expanded foam. The cardboard is peeled away from one side to reveal the smooth surface of the foam. By pressing into it with a small screwdriver, the effect of stone walls could be created. The walls at Tossa were time-worn, with some stones crumbling away, and the dented surfaces of these were easily produced on the model by simply depressing the surface of the foam for certain stones. The walls were colored by first painting a wash over the whole surface the color of the joints; then each stone was painted individually, varying the shades a little as she went. It sounds awful, but in practice it is an easy, relaxing and absorbing job.

To represent the pantiled roofs of the houses, she used foil pie plates and a specially made press to produce pantile shapes in a strip. There are many flights of steps ascending between the houses and stores, and these were more fiddly to make. The houses on one side of a flight were installed; then the styrofoam was roughly cut to shape, and the steps were formed from strips of cardboard.

Little rolling stock is available for the modeler of Spanish railroads, but fortunately Shirley tracked down a model Sharp Stewart locomotive of 1878 that passed into the ownership of the Madrid, Zaragoza and Andalucia Railway Company, and some "coast" coaches used on the coastal lines running from Barcelona. The pictures tell the rest of the story and show how amply her efforts were rewarded.

**BELOW**

**Big is not always best, as this little cameo shows. Even a simple plastic kit building placed in convincing surroundings and weathered well looks in keeping with the rest of the scene.**

# GLOSSARY

**Abutment** lateral support at the end of an arch or bridge.

**Adhesion** contact between wheel and rail.

**Ballast** material placed between crossties.

**Banking** assisting a train ascending a grade by attaching one or more locomotives at the rear.

**Cab control** operating one or more model trains singly or simultaneously.

**Cant** amount by which one rail or a curved track is raised above the other.

**Catenary** supporting cable for conductive wire of an overhead electrification system.

**Classification yard** place where cars are sorted and assembled into trains.

**Coal car** rail car that carries coal supplies in a separate, permanently coupled vehicle.

**Coupling** device for connecting vehicles together.

**Crosstie** or tie. Beam for supporting rails and holding them to the correct gauge.

**Diagram** display of trackwork and signals controlled by a signalbox.

**Distant signal** signal warning approaching trains about the state of stop signals ahead.

**End-to-end** layout with a terminal at either end.

**Flange** projecting rim on the inner side of a wheel.

**Freelance** a model not directly based on an actual prototype.

**Gauge** distance between rails of a track.

**Grade or gradient** slope or incline away from the horizontal.

**Halt** stopping place without station facilities for local lines.

**Headshunt** line running parallel with the main line for switching tracks.

**Home signal** semaphore stop signal.

**Hump yard** classification yard with artificial mound for the purpose of gravity sorting.

**Inspection saloon** Chief medical engineer's private coach.

**Island platform** platform with tracks on both sides.

**Joint bars** or fishplates. Metal or plastic insulated plates for joining lengths of rail together.

**Level crossing** where two tracks or a road and railroad cross at the same level.

**Light engine** locomotive without a train.

**Linesman** track maintenance man.

**Load gauge** the limiting height and width of rolling stock and loads to ensure adequate lineside clearance.

**Loop** continuous circular connection between up and down lines.

**Motor truck** truck with driving wheels or motorized axles.

**Multiple track** section of track with more than one up and one down line.

**Multiple unit** a "set" of cars internally powered by diesel or electric motors, operated by one driver.

**Narrow gauge** railway track of less than the standard gauge of 4 ft 8½ in.

**Packing** maintaining the correct tie level by adjusting the ballast beneath it.

**Pantagraph** link between overhead catenary system and the train or locomotive.

**Permanent way** track bed and tracks in position.

**Pilot** extra locomotive coupled to the front end of the train's locomotive to give it extra power for steep grades.

**Point** place at which trains can be directed onto another line.

**Pullman car** train car providing a high standard of comfort and service.

**Rail car** self-propelled passenger-carrying vehicle.

**Rolling stock** passenger and freight cars.

**Scenic break** a block in a layout to separate differing scenic backgrounds.

**Semaphore** type of signal with a pivoted arm that can be raised or lowered.

**Set back** reversing a train into a siding.

**Shay locomotive** gear-driven locomotive, driven by external shafts.

**Shuttle** regular round-trip service over a short route.

**Siding** line used to accommodate vehicles temporarily.

**Six-footway** area between parallel tracks.

**Solebar** main frame part of a car's underframe.

**Spike** wedge of wood or steel holding a rail in the tieplate bolted to the tie in position so it measures the correct gauge.

**Standard gauge** the measure of 4 ft 8½ in. between a pair of rails.

**Starter signal** signal giving authority for a train to proceed.

**Storage siding** set of sidings where trains are terminated and stored.

**Switch** to move vehicles onto a minor track or marshal vehicles into a particular order.

**Tank locomotive** locomotive that carries coal and water supplies on its own main frames.

**Terminal** end of the line or departure point, including station, switches, buildings, and other equipment.

**Tail light** light located at the rear of the last vehicle.

**Tie plate** metal castings, one on each end of the tie to hold it in place.

**Truck** short-wheelbase wagon with four or six wheels that can pivot at the center where it is attached to the underframe of a locomotive or car.

**Turntable** a rotating mechanism that turns locomotives around.

**Underbridge** underline bridge carrying trains over roads, rivers, and so on.

**Underframe** framework under the body of a rail car.

# INDEX